McGraw-Hill

WORKFORCE > career companion

HEALTH SCIENCE

Education

Bothell, WA • Chicago, IL • Columbus, OH • New York, NY

Image Credits: Cover Photo: Nicholas Rigg/Photographer's Choice RF/Getty Images.

www.mheonline.com

Copyright © 2012 by The McGraw-Hill Companies, Inc.

Send all inquiries to:
Contemporary/McGraw-Hill
130 E. Randolph St., Suite 400
Chicago, IL 60601

ISBN: 978-0-07-661071-6
MHID: 0-07-661071-3

Printed in the United States of America.

10 11 12 13 14 15 LHS 23 22 21 20 19 18

CAREER COMPANION
HEALTH SCIENCE

CONTENTS

TO THE STUDENT

EXPLORING AND PREPARING FOR A CAREER IN HEALTH SCIENCE

This resource booklet is designed to introduce you to the health science industry. It will tell you about the variety of jobs in the industry and how to build a career in this field. It will also provide the opportunity to practice the skills that will help you succeed in the industry. Explore the health science industry and practice the skills presented to help you decide if this industry is right for you.

Finding a job that interests you is the first step in managing your career. To be successful, however, you'll need to explore many job and career possibilities. What if your goals change? What if there is a shift in the labor market or the economy? You may need, or want, to change jobs or even careers. By improving your transferable skills, such as speaking, writing, organizing, planning, and problem solving, you will make yourself a more valuable employee and be able to cope with changes in the labor market. The more transferable skills you develop, the greater your chance of success at any job.

When considering a career in the health science industry, it is important to understand the realities of the industry. Which jobs have the strongest growth? Which offer good opportunities for advancement? Which jobs align most closely with your own abilities and interests? Are there many jobs available in your area?

Keep these questions in mind as you read Part I of this Career Companion booklet. When you have finished, refer to them again and see how many you can answer. Do the answers make you more or less likely to want to work in this industry? If you feel this industry may be right for you, work your way through the practice questions in Part II. Using real world situations, they will help you begin preparing for any career in the health science industry.

EXPLORE

This section of *Career Companion: Health Science* will introduce you to the health science industry.

You will explore the following topics:

THE HEALTH SCIENCE INDUSTRY

HEALTH SCIENCE JOBS

BUILDING A CAREER IN HEALTH SCIENCE

EDUCATION AND TRAINING

WORKING IN THE HEALTH SCIENCE INDUSTRY

INDUSTRY TRENDS

CAREER RESOURCES

After exploring this industry, you will be able to answer the following questions:

- What kinds of jobs are available in health science?
- How can I match my skills and interests with the right job?
- What are some important skills needed to work in health science?
- What is the work environment like?
- What factors affect trends in the industry?
- What resources can I use to find more information?

As you read this book, think about whether the careers described are right for you.

CHAPTER 1

THE HEALTH SCIENCE INDUSTRY

The health science industry, including both medical science and health care, provides a huge range of services. These include preventive care, surgery, counseling, and rehabilitation services. Through vaccines, screenings, and medications, health science has nearly wiped out diseases such as polio and measles. It has also helped treat illnesses such as cancer and AIDS.

Our lives are enriched by health science in other ways too. Research on nutrition and human development has improved human health. Research on common diseases such as diabetes has led to discoveries about healthy lifestyles.

Health science accounts for more than 14.3 million jobs. It is one of the largest industries in the United States. That number will increase as the baby boom population ages and develops health problems associated with getting older. And despite health care reform efforts, national spending on health care is expected to climb. The current spending is over $2.5 trillion.

Career Pathways in the Health Science Career Cluster

A **career cluster** is a grouping of jobs and industries based on common characteristics. A **career pathway** is an area of focus within a career cluster. Each pathway contains a group of careers requiring similar skills as well as similar certifications or education. The health science career cluster is divided into three main career pathways:

- **Diagnostic Services**

- **Therapeutic Services**

- **Support Services**

- **Health Informatics**

- **Biotechnology Research and Development**

The traditional health care setting is a hospital or a private practice. A private practice is a small medical business owned by one or more doctors. They may work in partnership with a hospital. But health care is being delivered in a wide range of locations. These facilities include clinics, treatment centers, diagnostic centers, nursing homes, and assisted-living facilities. In addition, home health agencies are bringing health care directly to patients' homes. People in this industry have more options than ever before in deciding where they will work.

DIAGNOSTIC SERVICES

Jobs in the diagnostic services pathway focus on diagnosing, or identifying, illness and disease. This is done by studying a patient's symptoms. Many workers in this pathway are technicians or technologists. They use X-rays, magnetic resonance imaging (MRIs), ultrasound, and other means to diagnose a patient. Others work as laboratory technicians.

Lab technicians draw blood and show patients how to collect other samples themselves. In a medical lab, they analyze tissue and bodily fluids. They may check blood sugar, cholesterol, and hormone levels. In medical research facilities, laboratory technicians help scientists investigate diseases.

Careers in diagnostic services require excellent observation skills for detecting and diagnosing symptoms. Workers must have outstanding listening skills so they can interpret patients' descriptions of their symptoms. They must have compassion so they can calm and comfort patients.

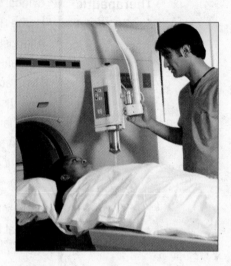

Nearly all workers in this pathway use high-tech equipment. They need both technical training and on-the-job training. Math and science skills are critical for success in most of these jobs. The ability to read and interpret printouts, charts, and gauges is important. Workers must be able to produce reports that give the results of the procedures they perform.

THERAPEUTIC SERVICES

Jobs in this career pathway focus on providing treatment and therapy. Workers treat both physical and emotional problems. Success in this pathway requires a desire to help people heal. It also requires patience, and compassion.

Many workers in this pathway are doctors and nurses. However, there are many other career options. These include jobs as physical therapists, home health aides, and emergency medical technicians (EMTs). Dietitians, dental hygienists, athletic trainers, and acupuncturists are also a part of this field.

All workers in this pathway need postsecondary education. The exact level of education varies according to the worker's responsibilities. Home health aides and dental hygienists need less formal education than nurses. Nurses must earn at least an associate's degree in nursing or a diploma from an accredited nursing school. Many nurses earn bachelor's and master's degrees so they can specialize within the pathway. Physicians and dentists must complete intensive postgraduate education and on-the-job training. They must also pass an exam to acquire a license to practice.

CAREER PATHWAY AND OCCUPATIONS	PROJECTED JOB OPENINGS 2008–2018
Diagnostic Services	
Radiologists #1	260,500
Cytotechnologists	53,300
Respiratory Therapists	41,400
Cardiovascular Technologists/Technicians	19,100
Diagnostic Medical Sonographers #2	16,500
Therapeutic Services	
Critical Care/Acute Care Nurses	1,039,000
Home Health Aides	552,700
Allergists and Immunologists	260,500
Dental Hygienists	98,400
EMTs and Paramedics	62,000
Low-Vision Therapists/Mobility Specialists	45,800
Dieticians/Nutritionists	25,700
Acupuncturists	15,300
Athletic Trainers	11,500
Support Services	
Patient Representatives	1,108,400
Mental Health/Substance Abuse Social Workers	61,300
Medical Equipment Repairers	23,200
Medical Equipment Preparers	11,200
Health Informatics	
Medical Secretaries	189,000
Medical Records and Health Information Technicians	70,300
Health Educators	26,000
Medical Transcriptionists	23,500
Biotechnology Research and Development	
Medical Scientists (except Epidemiologists)	66,200
Biomedical Engineers	14,900
Clinical Data Managers	9,600

Source: *O*NET Occupational Network Database*

SUPPORT SERVICES

Workers in this career pathway create a positive, helpful environment for patients and health care workers. Some workers in this pathway work closely with patients. Patient representatives help patients get the health care services they need. Social workers help people cope with mental health and substance abuse problems.

Others work in a variety of areas. Medical equipment technicians repair and maintain medical equipment. Occupational safety and health specialists work to prevent and minimize health hazards in the workplace. Environmental health specialists monitor air and water quality to ensure safety.

Support services careers employ workers with various levels of education. Some jobs require an associate's degree or bachelor's degree. Most workers in this career pathway need to be skilled with their hands, have good observation skills, and have the ability to use all the tools they need to do their jobs.

HEALTH INFORMATICS

Some of the fastest-growing jobs in this career cluster are in health informatics. Workers in this pathway are responsible for managing important health information. Some pass along health information to patients and the public. Others handle behind-the-scenes duties, from accounting to staffing.

Medical coders, medical billers, and medical claims processors make sure that health care providers are paid for their services. Educators share information that helps people manage or prevent health problems. Many workers focus on community-wide health and safety issues such as sexually transmitted diseases, smoking, and weight loss.

The level of education needed for careers in this pathway varies greatly depending on the job. Admitting clerks and patient service representatives must often have some college or technical training. Those in public health education typically have advanced degrees.

A career in health informatics requires a good memory, good organizational skills, and strong communications skills. Those who spend time working with the public and with patients should have good people skills. Workers who manage records and information should be detail-oriented.

BIOTECHNOLOGY RESEARCH AND DEVELOPMENT

Jobs in this pathway focus on the research and development of biotechnology, pharmaceuticals, and medical devices. Biotechnology is the application of science to create new medical advances, including the development of new drugs, vaccines, tests, and tissue-replacement procedures.

Biotechnology researchers work with the genetic materials of plants and animals. They may try to create new technologies and new treatments for disease. Geneticists, for example, study DNA and develop new techniques such as gene therapy. Pharmaceutical scientists focus on developing new medicines to treat diseases.

Workers in this pathway must have advanced scientific training, especially in biology and chemistry. They must also have good computer skills and be able to handle new technologies. Jobs in this pathway require attention to detail, excellent math skills, and analytical abilities.

Health Science Industry Outlook

The employment outlook for the health science industry is strong. By 2018, the industry will add 3.2 million positions. That represents a 22 percent increase from 2008. Job growth in the United States in general during that time is expected to be only 10 percent.

One factor driving job growth in the industry is the aging population. As people grow older, they face more health problems that require medical treatment. The success of medical science and technology is also triggering job growth. New cures, treatments, and medical devices are keeping people alive longer. Many more people will require care, therapy, and testing from the workers in the health science industry.

Rising health care costs are also increasing job growth in certain pathways. To keep costs down, some of the work traditionally performed by doctors, dentists, and other higher-paying positions is being done by people in lower-paying pathways. As a result, physician assistants, athletic trainers, physical therapy aides, dental hygienists, and others are among the country's 20 fastest-growing jobs.

Eleven of the fastest-growing occupations in the United States are in the health sciences. At the top of the list is biomedical engineering. There will also be fast job growth for home health aides and medical scientists.

HEALTH SCIENCE JOB OUTLOOK BY CAREER PATHWAY 2008–2018

PATHWAY	JOB OUTLOOK
Diagnostic Services	• Demand for respiratory therapists will continue to rise as older Americans develop more heart and lung diseases. • Cardiovascular (heart and blood vessel) technology is a fast-growing specialty. • Job growth in radiology is booming, with more than a 20 percent growth for radiologists and more than a 14 percent growth for radiological technologists.
Therapeutic Services	• Employment opportunities for doctors will continue to grow at a rapid pace. • Doctors interested in working in rural and low-income areas or in specialties that serve a high percentage of older patients will have even more employment options. • The number of job openings for registered nurses (RNs) between 2008 and 2018 is projected at more than 1 million. Supply is unlikely to keep up with demand. • Shorter hospital stays and the desire to recover or to be cared for at home is creating a demand for home health aides. Job growth is expected to rise more than 20 percent. • High turnover rates among nursing aides, orderlies, and attendants will create steady job opportunities.
Support Services	• The need for social workers specializing in serving patients with medical, mental health, substance abuse problems shows no signs of slowing down.
Health Informatics	• More health care providers are moving toward electronic health records (EHR), creating a demand for medical information technologists. • Despite advances in voice recognition software and EHR, physicians and other health care professionals will continue to need medical transcriptionists to create reports and summaries.
Biotechnology Research and Development	• Medical technology will fuel strong demand for biomedical engineers. • Biochemists and biophysicists will be in high demand due to intense interest in new drugs, vaccines, and treatments.

Source: US Department of Labor, *Career Guide to Industries 2010–11* and *O*NET Occupational Network Database*

HEALTH SCIENCE JOBS

The health science industry offers a huge variety of jobs. Many health care professionals work hands-on diagnosing, treating, counseling, and comforting patients. Some work in medical research laboratories, investigating diseases and developing new medicines. Others work behind the scenes, managing hospitals, processing health claims, and updating records. Here are some of the fastest-growing jobs in the health science industry and the skills they require.

CAREER PATHWAY ▶ Diagnostic Services

CARDIOVASCULAR TECHNOLOGIST AND TECHNICIAN

Cardiovascular technologists and technicians help doctors diagnose and treat heart and blood ailments. They schedule appointments, review files, and monitor the heart rates. They take care of equipment and explain procedures.

Many of these workers specialize in a specific type of technology. Some do invasive procedures, such as inserting a catheter into a patient's heart. Others may specialize in tests such as ultrasounds.

Special Skills Cardiovascular technologists and technicians must have mechanical skills and be able to follow detailed instructions. They should be able to put patients at ease with a pleasant, relaxed manner. They must be able to convey technical information to doctors.

RADIOLOGIST

People who take X-rays are known as a radiologists. They work with a range of diagnostic imaging technologies, including X-ray, ultrasound, magnetic resonance imaging (MRI), computed tomography (CT), and mammography.

Radiologist interpret the test results. They then communicate the results to the doctor. Radiologists may counsel patients on the risks and benefits of a procedure. In some cases, the radiologist may suggest alternative treatments.

Special Skills Radiologists must have technical knowledge and expertise. They must be able to use X-ray machines and other diagnostic imaging equipment. Workers should have a strong background in science and math. Strong observation skills are key to interpreting diagnostic images. Radiologists should have good people skills so they explain procedures and can put patients at ease.

CAREER PATHWAY ▶ Therapeutic Services

RESPIRATORY THERAPIST

A respiratory therapist helps patients who have breathing disorders. They work with a wide range of people, from asthma and emphysema sufferers to infants with underdeveloped lungs and patients on life support. They may work in hospitals or provide home care.

A respiratory therapist measures lung capacity by having the patient breathe into an instrument that measures the flow and volume of oxygen when breathing in and breathing out. If it shows that a patient is not getting enough oxygen, a respiratory therapist may remove mucus from the lungs, give the patient medication, provide an oxygen supply, or put the patient on a ventilator.

Special Skills Respiratory therapists work with patients as well as other medical staff. They must be able to provide clear, effective communication. Patients suffering from breathing disorders may experience feelings of suffocation and fear. Respiratory therapists should be caring and compassionate so they can put patients at ease. Since respiratory therapists often respond to emergencies, they must be able to work well under pressure.

OPTOMETRIST

An optometrist, or doctor of optometry (OD), is a doctor who examines the eyes for vision problems and diseases. Vision problems can affect visual accuracy, color perception, depth perception, and eye coordination. If an optometrist finds a problem with a patient's vision, he or she will develop a treatment plan. The plan may include prescription eyeglasses or contact lenses. Optometrists also prescribe drugs to treat eye problems. They do not perform eye surgery, but sometimes they provide pre- and post-operative care for cataracts. Most optometrists work in private practices, but some work in optical stores.

Special Skills Optometrists need thorough training in eye conditions and treatments. Those who choose to specialize in such areas as geriatrics (older people) or pediatrics (children) must undergo additional training. Good communication skills and attention to detail are also required. Optometrists who run their own businesses must have strong organizational skills.

PHYSICIAN ASSISTANT

A physician assistant (PA) is a licensed professional who practices medicine under the supervision of a doctor. PAs may work at private practices, hospitals, or nursing homes. They perform most of the duties of general practitioners. They conduct physical exams and provide preventive health care (care to prevent illness or disease). They also diagnose and treat illnesses, order and interpret tests, and assist in surgery. In most states, they can write prescriptions. Physician assistants may work in broad fields such as internal medicine or pediatrics, or they may specialize in surgery, orthopedics, or emergency medicine.

Special Skills Physician assistants must complete a recognized PA training program. These programs cover medical and behavioral sciences as well as clinical (hands-on) rotations in a variety of specialties. Physician assistants work closely with many other health care professionals. They should have excellent communication and teamwork skills. Physician assistants must take classes to keep up with advances in their field throughout their career, so self-motivation and a strong desire to learn are critical to success.

HOME HEALTH AIDE

Home health aides assist the sick, elderly, and disabled with household duties that these patients cannot perform alone. Aides work with patients on a very personal level, helping them bathe, use the bathroom, perform household chores, run errands, and move around their homes.

Aides also perform medical tasks such as monitoring heart rate, temperature, and breathing. They often change bandages and administer medication. Home health aides are often supervised by a registered nurse or physical therapist. They alert the supervisor to any changes in the patient's health or emotional well-being.

Special Skills Working as a home health aide requires a pleasant personality and good people skills. Aides provide support to patients. They must be kind, patient, and emotionally mature. Forming good relationships with patients can help patients heal and grow.

EMERGENCY MEDICAL TECHNICIAN/PARAMEDIC

Emergency medical technicians (EMTs) and paramedics are trained to provide emergency care to patients and to take patients to medical facilities. They are often the first people to arrive at emergency scenes. They work for private ambulance firms, hospitals, or fire departments.

The full range of emergency care that EMTs and paramedics can provide depends on their training. An EMT-1 provides basic emergency care. Those trained at the EMT-2 or EMT-3 level can give more advanced treatment. They may give patients intravenous fluids and use defibrillators to provide shocks to a heart that has stopped beating. EMT-4s, also known as paramedics, can use monitors and other equipment, and they can administer drugs.

Special Skills Emotional stability and the ability to make decisions quickly are essential for EMTs. In addition, EMTs and paramedics should be strong so they can lift people. When people are injured due to a crime, EMTs need good people skills to interact with victims as well as bystanders, witnesses, and victims' friends and family members. EMTs must be comfortable driving ambulances.

CAREER PATHWAY ▶ Support Services

PATIENT REPRESENTATIVE

Patient representatives work directly with patients and their families to explain a medical facility's policies, procedures, and services. They often serve as a connection between patients and medical or administrative staff to handle complaints, resolve problems, and clarify patients' rights issues. In addition, they may coordinate resources, handle phone inquiries, develop and distribute printed information, or even act as goodwill ambassadors in the hospital lobby.

Special Skills Top-notch people skills are essential, since patient representatives are often called upon to troubleshoot problems. Patient representatives need to be good listeners. They must quickly and effectively address patients' concerns—from wanting a phone in a hospital room to worrying about understanding a health care proxy. They should present a calm, friendly, professional demeanor at all times.

MENTAL HEALTH AND SUBSTANCE ABUSE SOCIAL WORKER

These social workers help improve the lives of patients with mental health and substance abuse issues. They may provide individual or group therapy. They may create plans to help patients readjust to everyday life when they leave the hospital. They may help people find jobs or deal with personal problems. Some social workers work in outpatient facilities. Outpatient facilities are places where patients come during the day for treatment.

Special Skills All social workers must be emotionally mature and objective in order to handle patients appropriately. They should be able to communicate well with people and be sensitive to people's problems. They should also be able to work independently and handle responsibility.

CAREER PATHWAY | Health Informatics

MEDICAL TRANSCRIPTIONIST

Medical transcriptionists are administrative workers who listen to dictation recorded by doctors. They transcribe, or record that information in writing, to create reports. Doctors (or other health care professionals) dictate these reports after examining patients or while interpreting diagnostic images and information, performing autopsies, or referring patients.

Transcriptionists edit the text they transcribe for grammar and clarity as they type. In order to accurately transcribe these tapes, medical transcriptionists must know the meaning and correct spelling of medical terms.

After reviewing and editing the text, medical transcriptionists return the transcribed information to the doctor for review and signature or for correction. These reports eventually become a part of a patient's medical records.

Special Skills Medical transcriptionists must have excellent word processing and computer skills as well as a comprehensive understanding of grammar and medical terminology. Good listening skills and attention to detail are also very important. Because they often work from home, medical transcriptionists must be self-motivated and organized.

INFORMATICS NURSE SPECIALIST

Informatics nurse specialists do not work with patients directly. Instead, they use their knowledge of nursing to help improve computerized health care systems. They may educate staff and help solve problems that arise in providing health care. They work to communicate nursing data and help health care workers and patients make decisions.

Special Skills Informatics nurse specialists must have excellent computer and other technology skills. They must be good problem solvers and be able to pull together a variety of information. They must also be able to communicate problems and solutions to staff.

Biotechnology Research and Development

CLINICAL DATA MANAGER

Clinical data managers oversee the collection, analysis, and reporting of data from clinical trials. Clinical trials are research studies conducted to determine the safety and effectiveness of new medical treatments. All prescription and over-the-counter medicines go through extensive clinical trials before their developers seek approval from the Food and Drug Administration (FDA). Clinical data managers are responsible for the accuracy, consistency, and completeness of the trial data. They must be familiar with complex data management programs. They must have math and technical skills so they can design trials.

Special Skills Clinical data managers typically have a background in statistics, computer science, and biology. They must be analytical thinkers with strong organizational skills so they can oversee large, lengthy projects. Since keeping accurate records is critical to success, clinical data managers should also be precise. Strong writing and speaking skills are also necessary for writing reports and presenting information to government regulatory agencies and to colleagues at the pharmaceutical companies and research institutes where they work.

BIOMEDICAL ENGINEER

Robotic arms, fiber optics used in arthroscopic surgery, pacemakers, and mammogram equipment would not be possible without biomedical engineers. Biomedical engineers are the inventors and innovators behind most technological advances in medicine. Not only do they design and develop products for people with disabilities, they also design and develop surgical tools and diagnostic equipment. Their work combines biology, medicine, and engineering. Demand for biomedical engineers is rising rapidly.

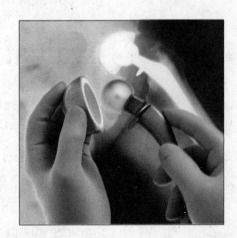

Special Skill Since designing new biomedical products requires careful and thorough testing at every stage of development, biomedical engineers require patience and the ability to do detailed work. They should be curious, creative problem solvers. The job requires good communication skills, since biomedical engineers often work in teams with other engineers and medical scientists. Biomedical engineers typically have at least a bachelor's degree in the field. However, many have advanced degrees and a strong knowledge of other engineering specialties.

BUILDING A CAREER IN HEALTH SCIENCE

Once you have chosen a field that interests you, look ahead and consider your career path. This path is made up of the job experiences and the career moves that lead you toward your career goal. You may take several steps before reaching your ultimate goal. You will likely spend time in an entry-level position. This will help you gain the professional experience necessary to move ahead in your career.

Many nurses, for example, start out as nursing assistants. As assistants, they get a first-hand look at nursing as a career. They learn how to interact with patients and how to do tasks such as moving patients and taking blood pressure. Nurses often get their training at a community college. After completing a two-year program, they take a test that qualifies them to be registered nurses. Later, a nurse may decide to do advanced study and become a nurse practitioner. Nurse practitioners often have specialities such as public health or pediatrics.

Don't worry if you change your mind about your career path. This happens to many people. It often takes time to find the right path. You can always change your career path regardless of where you are in your chosen profession.

Evaluating Career Choices

Choosing a career is challenging. Now is a good time to start thinking about what kind of career path you would like to follow. A well-chosen career can bring satisfaction and success in life.

Self-knowledge is the key to making wise career choices. Friends, teachers, and family members may offer helpful suggestions for potential careers. However, you are ultimately in charge of making your own career decisions.

Consider your personality, interests, aptitudes, and values when choosing a career. Think about why you chose to read this book. Of the many industries in which you could work, why does health science appeal to you?

You might feel that your personality, the way you think and behave, is suited to this industry. If you are a patient and compassionate person, a good listener, adept with technology, and drawn toward caring for others, then the health sciences may offer a good career choice.

You should also allow your interests to influence your career decisions. Are you interested in science? Would you enjoy volunteering at a local nursing home or hospital? People on the health science career path typically find themselves keeping up with the news on the latest advances in medical research and patient care.

In some cases, your aptitude, or ability in a certain area, will shape your career goals. Ask yourself what skills come naturally to you. An aptitude for data entry and a strong attention to detail might help you succeed as a pharmacy assistant or technician. However, aptitude is not the same as interest. You might be very good at math, but you might prefer a career that uses other skills.

Values are another factor to consider when selecting a career. Values are the principles and beliefs that you live by. You might value responsibility, compassion, courage, independence, or creativity. Your values will shape all areas of your life, from your long-term goals to the lifestyle you lead. For example, if being a responsible family member is important to you, you might seek a job that allows for flextime and provides good vacation benefits.

Success in the Health Science Career Cluster

As you have learned, the career opportunities in the health science industry are broad enough to accommodate workers with a variety of personality traits, interests, aptitudes, and values.

Your satisfaction with working in the health science industry will depend on how well you match yourself to a particular job. If you are uncertain about your desired career path, there are resources that can help. You can take self-assessment tests to find a career that matches your strengths. Part-time or temporary work can also help you discover your aptitudes and interests.

The careers profiled in this book represent just some of the types of jobs available in this industry. There are too many jobs to list in just one book. The workplace is constantly changing. Opportunities in traditional fields continue to expand, and new opportunities are constantly arising.

Learning about the range of job opportunities available to you will give you an advantage when you begin your job search. Developing workplace skills and learning about all aspects of the health science industry will also help you. As you make your career choices, think positively, keeping in mind your best attributes. Set ambitious but realistic goals, and keep an open mind about opportunities that may arise.

WORKING WITH DATA, PEOPLE, AND THINGS

Most careers offer opportunities to work with a combination of data, people, and things. Working with data involves the evaluation of information. Working with people requires building human relationships. Working with things involves using objects, such as tools, objects, and machines. Most jobs focus mainly on one of these. Researchers, for example, work mainly with data. Home health aides work primarily with people. Technicians work mostly with things. When planning your career path, consider what balance of data, people, and things you want in a career.

CAREERS THAT INVOLVE WORKING WITH DATA

Working with data means working with words, ideas, concepts, and numbers. Examples of working with data include organizing medical records, analyzing X-rays, and reporting the results of lab experiments.

Many people in health science work with data. Medical transcriptionists maintain patients' medical records and transcribe, or write down, information from doctors' recorded notes. Health care managers work with spreadsheets to analyze costs and profits. Doctors, nurses,  and therapists work with patient histories and medical information, read X-rays and charts, and keep records of their work.

Are you good with words and numbers? Do you enjoy applying scientific and mathematical principles to everyday situations? Do you grasp new concepts quickly? Do people say that you think logically? If so, you may want to consider a career that focuses on working with data.

CAREERS THAT INVOLVE WORKING WITH PEOPLE

All jobs in health science involve working with people—coworkers, managers, administrators, technicians, patients, and patients' families. Because everyone needs health care at some time, health science workers interact with people from every possible cultural, economic, and language background.

To succeed in their careers, most health science workers need good people skills. Pediatricians spend their days diagnosing and treating sick children. Dental hygienists clean patients' teeth, take X-rays, and assist dentists. Nursing aides help patients bathe, eat, and get dressed. Home health care workers provide emotional support to homebound patients. Registered nurses examine patients, arrange treatment plans, and provide follow-up evaluations. Public health workers speak at conventions, meetings, and clinics to educate the public about timely health care issues. Physical therapists devise treatment plans for injured patients working on recovery. In short, nearly everyone who works in health science works with people.

People who enjoy working with people are generally outgoing. To decide if you are a "people person," ask yourself a few questions. Do you place great emphasis on your friendships with others? Do you spend your spare time socializing with friends or family? Are you good at judging the motivations and feelings of others? If so, you'll probably enjoy a job that allows for frequent interaction with others.

CAREERS THAT INVOLVE WORKING WITH THINGS

Health science includes many jobs that focus on working with things. Examples of working with things include dispensing medicine, operating and repairing medical equipment, and using precision tools such as scalpels and drills.

Many workers in health science, even those who spend most of their time working with people, spend some time working with things. For example, laboratory technicians use equipment such as microscopes and centrifuges. Patient care assistants handle thermometers, specimen collection tools, and blood pressure cuffs.

Think about how you choose to spend your spare time. Do you enjoy building or repairing things? Are you curious about how artificial limbs work? Do you prefer to work with your hands? If so, you're probably well suited for working with things.

DATA, PEOPLE, AND THINGS IN THE HEALTH SCIENCE INDUSTRY

Whatever career in health science you choose, you're likely to spend some time working with data, people, and things. Choosing a job that matches what you like to do will make you a better employee and a happier person.

To find a job that best suits your strengths, browse jobs listed in the Dictionary of Occupational Titles (www.occupationalinfo.org). Each job has a nine-digit code that describes it. The fourth, fifth, and sixth digits show how much each job involves working with data, people, and things. The lower the number, the more complex the particular type of work. For example, a pharmacist assistant's code is 074.381.010. The numbers 3, 8, and 1 mean complex work with data, less complex work with people, and very complex work with things.

Finding Employment

Finding a job is seldom easy, but finding a job in a new career field can be especially hard. Whether you have a job or are unemployed, now is a good time to explore new careers and make yourself more interesting to employers.

CHANGING CAREERS

Many people jump from one career right into another. They may feel that their job does not match their skills or interests. They may believe the job does not offer enough room to advance. A new career can offer new opportunities.

The best time to think about a new career is when you are already employed. While you have a job, there is less pressure to find a new job right away. Investigate which career fields have good opportunities in the area where you live. Think about your current job. What aspects of the job do you enjoy? Which other careers that involve similar tasks?

If you find a job that you would like to pursue, spend time investigating the qualifications required. You might speak to someone who works in the industry. Learn as much as you can to ensure the career cluster is right for you.

Look for ways you can gain experience that will help you in your search. If the new career involves working with people, volunteer for tasks in which you will interact with people.

You should spend time creating a résumé. Use print and online resources to learn how to create the résumé that best highlights your qualifications. Highlight the skills that are most relevant to the jobs you will apply for. You should also spend time networking, or reaching out to people who can help in your job search. This may include family, friends, or colleagues from current or former jobs. Make an effort to meet new people to expand your network. One good way to do this is to use online networking sites.

UNEMPLOYMENT

Being unemployed can be a difficult time, but it can bring new opportunities. Millions of people are unemployed at any time, so there is no shame in being unemployed. If you find yourself unemployed, be sure to apply for unemployment benefits. Benefits are given only after you are approved, so be sure that you apply right away.

Make the most of your time while you are unemployed. Work on your résumé. Expand your network. Try to stick to a daily schedule. For example, you might shower and dress as if going to work and then spend the morning crafting your résumé or searching for jobs. Rather than spending every waking hour looking for work, set aside some time for leisure activities.

Consider finding a freelance or part-time job that can help you gain new skills and earn more money while you search. You might also take a class that teaches skills useful in a new career.

CHAPTER 4

EDUCATION AND TRAINING

Jobs in health science require varying levels of education and training. Many jobs in this industry require little or no formal training. For others, it is necessary to have specific education and experience.

Training and Education for Health Science

The level of training needed to succeed in health science varies by career. Jobs can be categorized into three groups—those requiring little or no training, those requiring some training, and those requiring advanced training.

Jobs that involve diagnosing and treating patients (for example, physician, surgeon, optometrist, physical therapist) require four years of college followed by many years of postgraduate education and training. Support positions, such as those that assist in patient care, perform diagnostic tests, and maintain health science records, often call for little more than on-the-job training.

JOBS REQUIRING LITTLE OR NO TRAINING

Many health science jobs require little or no formal training. Examples include receptionist, orderly, housekeeper, and ambulance driver. Many patient-care jobs also require no previous training. Training for jobs such as nurse assistant, home health aide, and physical therapy assistant is usually provided by the employer when you are hired.

Where health science workers are in shorter supply, people with little previous experience or training may be able to work as aides. Nursing homes, psychiatric care facilities, and home health care services often provide on-the-job training. Some also offer classroom instruction.

However, getting a high school education or the equivalent is important. Many employers look for workers who earned solid grades in high school. Failing to complete high school may hurt your chances for advancement.

JOBS REQUIRING SOME TRAINING

Many jobs in the health sciences require specialized training. Examples include paramedics, nurses, and assistants in dental, medical, and pharmacy settings.

People can receive education and training in a variety of ways. Community colleges, junior colleges, and four-year institutions offer certificates, associate's degrees, and bachelor's degrees in health science fields. Online education through an accredited provider is also a popular way to earn a degree.

Many trade organizations offer certification programs. Trade organizations represent a specific industry or type of job. Certification by a trade organization verifies training in a specific occupation.

Earning an associate's degree, certificate, or professional certification can help you advance in your field. For information about such programs, contact trade organizations or community colleges and technical schools in your area. You can learn about trade organizations by visiting the websites listed on page 38.

TRAINING REQUIRED FOR HEALTH SCIENCE JOBS

Jobs Requiring Little or No Training

Dietetic Technicians	Nurse Assistant/Aides/Orderlies and Attendants
Dental Laboratory Technicians	
Home Health Aides	Medical Receptionists
Medical Equipment Preparers	Pharmacy Aides

Jobs Requiring Some Training or Education

Dental Assistants	Medical Laboratory Technicians
Dental Hygienists	Medical Transcriptionists
Emergency Medical Technician	Nurses, all areas
Medical Assistants	Paramedics
Medical Equipment Repairers	Pharmacy Technicians

Jobs Requiring Advanced Training or Education

Athletic Trainers	Mental Health and Substance Abuse Social Workers
Biologists	
Biomedical Engineers	Nurse Practitioners
Clinical Data Managers	Occupational Therapists
Dietitians and Nutritionists	Orthotists
Dentists	Physicians, all areas
Medical and Public Health Social Workers	Pharmacists
	Radiologists

SOURCE: US Department of Labor, *Dictionary of Occupational Titles* and *Occupational Handbook 2010–2011*

JOBS REQUIRING ADVANCED TRAINING

Many health science jobs require an advanced degree. Some jobs also require an internship or a residency. Read on for more information on degree offerings.

Pre-Employment Training

Employers often favor job candidates with credentials that exceed minimum requirements. Consider dental hygienists and radiation therapists. They only need an associate's degree to work in their chosen career. However, they may be competing against candidates with bachelor's and master's degrees.

More education provides greater skills, increased responsibility, and improved opportunities. It can also increase your pay rate. More education allows you to perform a wider variety of tasks, so it may make your work more interesting.

Depending on your career choice, pre-employment training may require an associate's degree or certificate, a bachelor's degree, postgraduate education, an internship, a license, or a certificate.

ASSOCIATE'S DEGREES AND CERTIFICATES

An associate's degree requires completing a two-year program at a community college or technical school. For example, a two-year program for health information technicians teaches basic life sciences, medical terminology, and ethics. It also covers the health care system, statistics, and information science and technology. Students who complete the program are qualified to work as medical coders, medical records technicians, and medical abstracters.

Certificate programs may also be offered by some institutions. Earning a certificate demonstrates knowledge and ability needed in a specific occupation. Certificate programs usually do not require general education classes. Because of this, a certificate can often be earned in less time than an associate's degree.

Some programs have a hands-on component. Dental hygiene and veterinary technician programs, for example, require many hours of direct patient care in addition to educational classes.

A technical school is option for positions that call for one or two years of training. Technical schools offer programs in a number of industries, including health care. For example, a technical school program for occupational therapy assistants will teach treatment options and activities, creativity, and problem-solving skills. This training can lead to certification or an associate's degree.

BACHELOR'S DEGREE

A bachelor's degree is earned after completing a four-year program at a college or university. Most technologists, mid-level administrators and managers, and educators need bachelor's degrees. Jobs that require bachelor's degrees call for greater technical knowledge than associate's degree programs provide. They carry more administrative responsibility and demand excellent problem-solving skills.

Before choosing a postsecondary educational (study conducted after high school) program, consider the length of the program and its rate of job placement. Find out whether the program is nationally accredited. Take into consideration the school's reputation in the field.

Another important factor is cost. You may be able to finance your education through loans, grants, work-study programs, and scholarships. Contact the school's financial aid office to find out which scholarships you might qualify for.

POSTGRADUATE EDUCATION

Postgraduate education is conducted after the completion of a bachelor's degree. Most people who seek postgraduate education enroll in master's or doctoral degree programs.

A master's degree requires completing an additional one- to three-year program on a specific subject. Many therapists, health care administrators, and advanced technologists hold master's degrees. Doctoral degrees are the highest academic degrees. They require at least five (and as many as seven) years of postgraduate study, hands-on experience, and independent research.

INTERNSHIPS

Internships offer supervised, hands-on experience. Interns often receive little or no pay. However, the experience they gain greatly improves their chances of landing a paying job. Internships may lead to a license, certificate, or degree in health science. For example, music therapists must complete a 1,000-hour supervised internship before receiving their undergraduate degrees.

LICENSING

A license is official recognition by a state government that a person meets requirements to practice a certain profession. Licensing protects the public from practitioners with inadequate knowledge and skills or fake credentials.

Licenses are usually required for workers responsible for the health and safety of others. Licensing requirements can vary by state, and some professions also have national licensing standards. For example, nurses must pass a national licensing examination and fulfill state requirements.

CERTIFICATION

Certification is an official recognition of a worker's skill in a specific job. Certifications are issued by professional organizations. They usually require education, workplace experience, and passing a standardized test. Certifications are valued by employers because they show mastery of skills. Certification as a nephrology clinical technician, for example, demonstrates that a person has the skills needed to work at a dialysis center.

Job and Workplace Skills

When considering job candidates, employers look for both job-specific skills and general workplace skills. Job-specific skills are the skills necessary to do a particular job. They may include operating a medical device or understanding the human body. General workplace skills can be used in a variety of jobs.

HEALTH SCIENCE SKILL STANDARDS

The National Consortium for Health Science Education has a list of skill standards for the health science industry. Here are some skills that relate to specific career pathways:

- **Therapeutic Service** Workers in this pathway should have strong communication skills and be able to work well with a team. They must be able to create and implement a treatment plan. They should be able to monitor patients and evaluate their progress.

- **Diagnostic Services** Workers in this pathway should have strong communication skills. They should be able to assess the health of patients. They should be able to conduct, evaluate, and report on procedures that are requested.

- **Health Informatics** Health informatics workers should be able to manage the flow of communication. They should be able to analyze and interpret health information and records. They must develop processes for sharing information and understand what information is private.

- **Support Services** These workers should be able to implement department goals and policies and to coordinate activities with other departments. They should be able to monitor the quality of care and make sure all regulations are being met. Workers must help keep a clean workplace and ensure that resources are being used effectively.

- **Biotechnology Research and Development** Workers in this pathway should understand the importance of research in improving people's quality of life. They should be highly skilled in math, genetics, chemistry, and biology. Workers should understand specific biotechnology processes and lab procedures. They should know how new products are designed. Finally, they should understand the ethics involved in their work.

Other skills relate generally to the health science career cluster. Some of these skills include the following:

Academic Foundations Health science workers need well-developed academic skills. These include knowledge of the human body and its functions and understanding of diseases and disorders. They also include basic math skills related to health care procedures.

System Knowledge Health science workers need to know their role within the health system. This means understanding their contribution to their department and the entire workplace. They must understand how various health science professionals work together to provide care. They should also have a basic understanding of how health care is delivered and how it is paid for.

Legal Responsibilities Health science workers must understand the legal responsibilities and limitations of their job. They must be aware of the possible consequences of their actions. They must follow workplace and legal regulations, policies, and laws. This includes reporting accidents, keeping patient records private, and following workplace safety standards and laws.

Ethics Ethics are the values that help people know right from wrong. All health science workers must understand accepted ethical practices in health science. They must respect the ethical standards of different cultures and ethnicities. Additionally, they have to understand and accept differences between their own personal ethics and the ethics of their organization.

Safety Practices Health science workers need to understand potential health and safety hazards. Infection-control and work-safety procedures are in place to protect them, other workers, and patients from injury and illness. They need to follow all health and safety recommendations and use safe work practices.

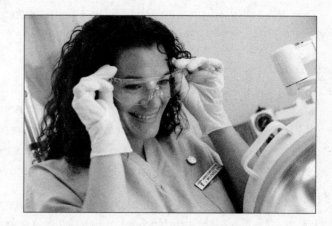

Health Maintenance Practices Health science workers must know the fundamentals of wellness and disease prevention so they can encourage healthy living. They need to learn about behaviors that promote good health, including routine health screenings, regular checkups, and alternative medicine.

Technical Skills Health science workers must have the technical skills they need to perform their workday duties. They need to learn to measure and record vital signs, recognize "normal" ranges, and perform cardiopulmonary resuscitation (CPR).

Information Technology Applications Health science workers must understand the information technology used in their careers. They should be able to identify records and files, access and distribute data, and recognize technology applications in health science settings.

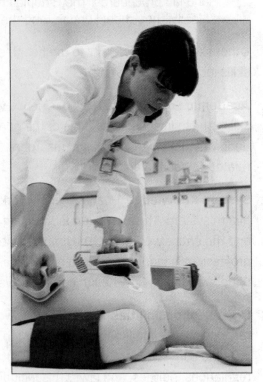

CORE SKILLS

Core skills differ from academic or job-specific skills. Acquired both inside and outside the classroom, they are useful in any career. Strong core skills make you more marketable in any job or industry.

Communication Oral and written communication skills are important in any health science job. Health science workers interact with a wide range of people. They need to communicate clearly and adapt their communication style to each patient's or coworker's style.

Listening Skills Health science workers must listen to and understand their patients' descriptions of symptoms. Failing to listen to a patient could cause a serious physical or emotional problem to be overlooked. Good listening skills are also needed to properly address patients' worries or concerns, follow workplace instructions, and understand coworkers' ideas or points of view.

Body language and tone of voice can be as important as the words spoken. Pay attention not only to what a person says, but also to how the person says it.

Problem-Solving Skills Employers value workers who can recognize problems and find solutions. Many health science jobs involve almost constant problem solving. For example, hospital administrators spend their days solving budget issues or addressing problems with staff, patients, and programs.

Decision-Making Skills Making good decisions requires you to identify goals, generate alternatives, gather information, and make judgments. Health science workers make important decisions every day. For example, paramedics assess the condition of the patient, choose a treatment, and decide when to call for more help.

Organizing and Planning Skills Planning requires setting goals and identifying the steps required to realize them. The ability to organize and plan is especially important when managing teams. For example, a nursing supervisor directing the nursing staff coordinates nursing service activities and schedules orientations and training.

Teamwork Skills Teamwork is key in any health science career. Good team members know how to compromise, complete tasks on time, and value the ideas and contributions of others. Conflict resolution skills are also helpful. For example, the head of a research team may need to agree to a decrease the amount of money requested for a project while keeping the team motivated and committed.

Social Skills Social skills comprise a wide range of abilities, from leadership skills to simply showing respect for those around you. Social skills are essential for putting patients at ease and developing good working relationships with other employees.

Technology Skills No matter what your job is, you'll likely use some form of technology every workday. Computers, medical technology, and telecommunications equipment are all used in health science to improve efficiency and response time. As equipment becomes more advanced, workers must adapt to upgrades and learn new computer programs.

Adaptability Skills Health science is a fast-changing industry. Advances in technology, scientific discoveries, and economic changes require workers to adapt. Job responsibilities can change from year to year, or even day to day. For example, a physician assistant working an emergency room shift might sew up a wound, help deliver a baby, and assess an accident victim for internal injuries. Workers in this industry must be ready to acquire new skills. Being able to change increases a worker's chance of employment.

CHAPTER 5

WORKING IN THE HEALTH SCIENCE INDUSTRY

When choosing a career path, it is important to know what it is like to work in the industry. Understanding the work environment, hazards, and benefits of a job can help you make informed decisions.

Work Environment

Work environment refers to factors that affect workers' health and satisfaction on the job. These include the physical surroundings and the working hours. They also include the physical activities required to perform the job.

PHYSICAL ENVIRONMENT

The work environment in health science varies by job. Surgeons, physicians, and nurses may work in busy hospitals or private practices. Medical and dental technicians spend their days in clean, sterile laboratories. Paramedics and emergency medical technicians spend their days in ambulances or fire trucks, driving to medical emergencies. They must treat patients in all types of weather, indoors or outdoors. In most cases, however, workers in this industry work in clean, well-lit, and well-supplied environments.

WORK HOURS

The work hours of health science jobs also vary widely. Some health workers, such as dentists and doctors, often run their own practices and can set their own hours. However, they may need to be on call to treat emergencies. For example, surgeons are often asked to be on call to treat patients in hospital emergency rooms. If someone needs surgery while the surgeon is on call, the surgeon must leave for the hospital immediately.

Many people in the health science industry work long hours. Emergency medical technicians often work 50 hours a week. Doctors may work even more hours.

Since hospitals and medical care facilities must always be available to the public 24 hours a day, many workers in health science work in shifts. Shift work is common for medical personnel such as doctors, nurses, and paramedics. Shift work divides the day into blocks of time, generally eight-hour blocks. But it is not uncommon for health professionals to work 12-hour or even 24-hour shifts.

WORKING CONDITIONS IN HEALTH SCIENCE

Diagnostic Services

- Radiologists must have good physical stamina to be able to stay on their feet and move disabled patients.
- Radiologists must wear lead aprons, gloves, and other devices to avoid being exposed to radiation.
- Clinical laboratory personnel must wear masks, gloves, and goggles to avoid infection. They spend most the day on their feet.
- Many clinical laboratory personnel work shifts, including evening and weekend shifts; some need to be on call.

Therapeutic Services

- Some physicians work in small offices that have limited administrative support, while others work in larger offices that are part of a health care group.
- Surgeons must be alert and physically fit, as surgery often requires standing for many hours.
- Many physicians work long, irregular hours and are on call for emergency services and patient consultations.
- Shift work, including weekend, night, and holiday shifts, is typical for many doctors and nurses.
- Life-or-death situations and frequent exposure to sick and injured people can make the job stressful.
- Most dentists work in solo practices; they usually work four or five days a week.
- Dental hygienists usually have flexible hours.
- EMTs and paramedics work in hospital emergency rooms and on ambulances; they may be outdoors in all types of weather.
- Many health practitioners, including pharmacists, chiropractors, and nurse practitioners, are on their feet most of the day.
- Home health care workers are at risk for back strain and other injuries associated with lifting and moving patients.

Support Services

- Many medical and health service managers work long hours.
- Dietetic technicians often work in clean, well-ventilated areas, but others work in hot, congested kitchens. They may spend most of the day on their feet.

Health Informatics

- Medical transcriptionists generally work in comfortable settings. Many work from home offices.
- Medical records and health information specialists may work day, evening, or night shifts.

Biotechnology Research and Development

- Clinical data managers generally work normal hours in an office environment.

Source: US Department of Labor, *Career Guide to Industries 2010–11* and *O*NET*

Many health science employees may need to work overtime. Overtime is work time beyond 40 hours a week. Because hospitals are open around the clock, most doctors, nurses, specialists, and staff such as admitting clerks work some nights, weekends, and holidays. Most health care managers often work overtime. They may spend time traveling.

ESSENTIAL PHYSICAL ACTIVITIES

Many occupations in the health science industry require hands-on activities. Some are unique to this career cluster. For example, doctors, nurses, and some technicians must draw blood from patients. They must handle specimens safely and carefully. These duties require the workers to be skilled with their hands.

Many workers in health science spend all day on their feet. Nurses spend most of their shifts standing and walking. They perform many physical activities such as moving patients, moving medical equipment, and changing bedding.

Other health care workers may move patients or heavy equipment. These include home health aides, paramedics, ambulance drivers, physician assistants, doctors, and radiologic technologists. These workers must be physically fit and trained in the proper procedures to avoid injury to patients.

Ambulance drivers, EMTs, and home health care workers must drive carefully to protect themselves and patients from accidents and injuries. Surgeons must have very steady hands and good vision, and they must be able to work with extreme care and precision for many hours. Dentists must be able to work carefully within the confines of a person's mouth.

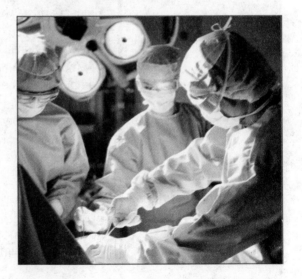

Hazards and Environmental Dangers

Because accidents can happen on any job, safety must always be a priority. The federal government protects workers by creating workplace safety standards and laws. These rules help prevent accidents and ensure that accident victims are offered assistance.

INJURIES AND ILLNESSES

Most on-the-job impairments are either occupational injuries or occupational illnesses. An occupational injury is any injury that occurs at work. Injuries include cuts, fractures, and sprains. An occupational illness is caused by on-the-job exposure to harmful substances. These illnesses include rashes and skin diseases, respiratory problems, or poisoning.

Workers in health science face unique dangers. They must take special precautions to avoid catching or spreading infectious diseases. Workers in this industry often come into contact with blood and other bodily fluids. They are also in contact with patients who may have contagious diseases. Workers may be exposed to illnesses as minor as the common cold or as dangerous as AIDS, hepatitis, and tuberculosis. Clothing such as latex gloves, masks, and gowns help protect workers and patients from disease.

In addition, workers must always be careful when handling needles. They must ensure that they do not prick themselves or someone else. Needles, bodily tissue and fluids, and other hazardous materials must always be disposed of properly so these items do not spread diseases.

Radiologic technologists are often exposed to radiation. They must take precautions to protect themselves. Radiation exposure can be limited by using lead aprons, gloves, and shields. These workers also must wear special badges that measure radiation levels while they are at work. Finally, they must ensure that patients are not exposed to too much radiation.

RATES OF WORK-RELATED INJURIES AND ILLNESSES IN THE HEALTH SCIENCE INDUSTRY PER 100 FULL-TIME WORKERS (2009)

Occupation	Rate
Nursing and residential care facilities	11.1
Hospitals (state government)	11.0
Nursing and Residential care facilities	8.4
Hospitals	7.3
Hospitals (local government)	7.0
Social assistance	4.0
Administrative and support services	2.7
Ambulatory health care services	2.7
Professional, scientific and technical services	1.2

Source: US Department of Labor

ERGONOMICS

Developments in ergonomics are helping create a healthier work environment. Ergonomics is the study of how to design a workplace environment to make it safer and more comfortable. Ergonomic workstations, for example, can be adjusted to accommodate workers of different heights. They can reduce hand and arm movements, promote healthful body posture, and reduce physical stress. One goal of ergonomics is to reduce the occurrence of disorders such as repetitive stress injuries (RSIs), which can occur when a person performs the same motion many times.

RSIs are common among administrators and technicians. One of the most common RSIs is carpal tunnel syndrome. This is a swelling of tendons in the wrist, which can result from frequent repetition of tasks such as typing. Medical coders, billers, and transcriptionists are most likely to suffer from RSIs because they work at keyboards for most of the day.

Recently companies have been working to develop ergonomically correct devices for surgeons, doctors, and dentists to help cut down on injuries. New tools decrease stress on the hands and arms. Modern equipment is adjustable, which makes it more comfortable to use. This reduces the need for the reaching and grabbing movements that can lead to repetitive stress injuries.

Job Benefits

Benefits aren't just extras. They not only make your life easier and safer, but they can also be worth 20 to 35 percent of your salary.

Standard job benefits usually include paid health insurance, holidays, sick time, and vacations. At most companies, new employees do not start receiving paid vacation time until they have been on the job for 90 days or more. The specific job benefits you receive will depend on several factors, such as the size and type of organization you work for is one how many years you have been on the job.

At some companies, job benefits have expanded in recent years to include more than health insurance, paid vacation, and holidays, and sick leave. Some expanded benefits may include the following:

- dental, life, and disability insurance

- time off to care for sick children

- tuition assistance

- 401(k) plan, or a retirement plan in which employees invest a portion of their income and employers match the contribution

Labor Unions

A union is a group of workers who unite to bargain for job improvements. Union leaders negotiate with company management for better wages, increased benefits, better working conditions, and other job improvements. If an agreement is not reached, the union may use its most powerful tool—a strike. A strike occurs when employees stop working in an effort to force an employer to agree to the union's terms. In most cases, unions maintain strike funds, which provide partial salaries to striking workers.

When an agreement is reached between the union and company management, the company signs a labor contract. A labor contract is a legal agreement specifying wages, work hours, working conditions, and benefits. The union members must approve the contract before it goes into effect.

UNIONS IN THE HEALTH SCIENCE INDUSTRY

Unions, though still powerful, have declined in membership since World War II. In the health science industry, less than 15 percent of workers belong to unions.

Union membership varies by setting. Union workers are common in hospitals, but most workers in physician offices do not belong to unions. In recent years, some unions have united in the hopes of growing stronger. For example, in 2009 four nursing unions combined to form National Nurses United, which became the largest union for registered nurses.

If you join a union, you will be asked to pay an initiation fee and dues. This money supports the strike fund and the work of the union. If you are thinking about joining a union, consider the membership cost and the benefits. You should also consider what the union has accomplished on behalf of its members in the past. In some occupations, you may be required to join a union as a condition of employment.

CHAPTER 6

INDUSTRY TRENDS

The health science career cluster is constantly evolving. Advances in technology affect how health care can be provided to people. The changing population and its needs also create new trends in the industry.

Technology in the Health Science Industry

Technology has changed the health science industry in many ways. These changes have led to new and better ways to diagnose, treat, and prevent illness. Doctors now use technology to communicate with paramedics to assess patients' conditions before the ambulance arrives at the hospital. Tests that were once done in labs can now be run in an ambulance or even at home.

Some of these changes have also made health science more environmentally friendly. Electronic health records, accessible through computers and hand-held devices, have reduced the amount of paper used. The increase in health care done through the Internet has reduced the need to drive to doctors' offices. Hospitals have begun using "green information technology" such as cloud computing, or virtual servers, to reduce the amount of computer hardware used.

SMARTPHONES

Most doctors now routinely use smartphones and tablet computers in their work. These devises allow doctors to access and convey information from anywhere. They may look up information about drugs and procedures, play instructional videos for patients, or write electronic prescriptions. Doctors can instantly receive test results and immediately change patient treatment.

Using a smartphone or a table computer is more convenient than using a computer. Hospital health workers can keep these small devises in their pockets as they move from room to room. Hundreds of smartphone applications have been developed for medical workers.

MEDICAL INFORMATICS

Medical informatics is the study of using medical information, such as patient records and research data, for decision making and problem solving. Workers in this field try to make patient care, medical research, and health care administration more effective. As technology advances, medical informatics is becoming more and more important in health science.

One important application of medical informatics is the use of computerized systems for storing patient information. Many hospitals and practices now compile and store patient medical records electronically.

Patients' records are updated whenever patients seek medical treatment. Information, such as lab test results, allergies, prescriptions, and vital signs, is added to the record. This gives a comprehensive portrait of the patient's health. Some doctors use smartphones or computers to input information directly into a patient's record during a consultation. Some computerized devices, such as MRI machines, can even feed data directly into the patient's record.

Many electronic record systems have multimedia capabilities. They can store photographs, voice recordings, and videos. They can also organize information, suggest ways of assessing patients, and provide alerts to health workers. Some systems are connected to many hospitals.

These record systems give health professionals immediate access to patient information. They can help doctors diagnose patients by showing them the patient's full medical picture. They can learn about recurring symptoms and past illnesses. The systems can also help administrators manage patient records, set up appointments, and verify insurance information.

TELEMEDICINE

Another growing field in health science technology is telemedicine. Telemedicine is the use of technology to connect patients with medical services and information.

Telemedicine is being used in many settings. It allows school nurses to consult with physicians. It helps homebound patients to communicate with doctors, and it allows prisons to provide health services to inmates who cannot be transported.

Telemedicine consultations are based on three types of technology. The first method, known as store and forward, enables the transfer of digital images from one location to another. In this system, the doctor and patient exchange information but don't hold live virtual meetings. A worker might use e-mail to send images and sounds of an abnormal heart to a cardiologist for a diagnosis. Store and forward is used in situations when a diagnosis is necessary but not urgent.

The second method involves monitoring a patient remotely. Devices at a patient's home might record data, such as blood pressure or glucose levels. That information is then automatically sent to a physician, nurse, or other health worker.

The third method of telemedicine is interactive services. Health workers and patients can hold virtual meetings, using video or web-based conferences.

MINIMALLY INVASIVE SURGICAL TECHNOLOGIES

Today's surgical technologies focus on making surgery less invasive and less traumatic to the body. Using lasers or high-intensity focused ultrasound instead of scalpels, surgeons can operate on patients without cutting tissue. Surgeons can even perform noninvasive surgery on brain tumors by using radiation to kill unwanted cells.

Minimally invasive surgeries are faster and less risky than regular surgeries. They are less painful, require less healing time, and often do not require anesthesia. Two techniques gaining in popularity are laser surgery and robotic surgery.

Laser surgery is the use of a laser instead of knife to cut tissue or remove bleeding blood vessels. Unlike a scalpel, a laser heats cells in tissue until they burst. The laser works by breaking the bonds of molecules that hold the tissue together, without damaging the tissue. Laser surgery has found numerous applications, including the removal of tumors, varicose veins, and even tattoos. Surgeons use different kinds of lasers to perform different types of surgery.

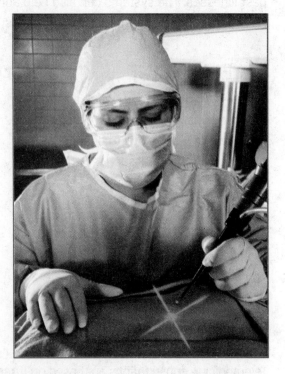

Robotic surgery is surgery performed by remote-controlled robotic devices. Surgeons use remote controls and voice-activated software to guide robotic devices through specific surgical tasks. One of the most important benefits of robotic surgery is that it is minimally invasive. Because only tiny cuts are required, healing time is much faster. Surgical robots can be steadier and more precise than even the best surgeon.

DENTAL TECHNOLOGIES

In many dental offices, traditional dental tools are being replaced with high-tech equipment. This equipment is often designed to be more effective and less painful for patients. Tools using air abrasion are increasingly used in place of dental drills. Air abrasion is the use of compressed air to blow tiny particles onto teeth. It gets rid of tooth decay as well as stains on tooth enamel. Air abrasion is less painful than traditional drilling procedures. It is silent, and it produces no vibration.

Lasers are also beginning to be used in dentistry. Some dentists use lasers to remove decay in teeth and remove tissue to test for cancer. They can also be used to reshape gums and whiten teeth.

Workplace Trends in Health Science

Workplace trends affecting the health science field include the use of consultants, medical consultations, and temporary workers.

Consultants A consultant provides specialized services for one or more clients. Consultants are sometimes called in when a new project starts or a system is re-evaluated. Some consultants work for one client on a long-term project. Others work for several clients at once. A health care manager, for example, may be called in to establish new hospital procedures. As a result of a recent dramatic increase in medical malpractice lawsuits, medical expert witnesses are in growing demand.

Medical Consultations Perhaps the most common form of consultation, or meeting of professionals, is the interaction between specialists. Doctors specializing in one area of medicine consult with doctors in another area. They work together to determine the best course of action for a patient. This form of consultation gives doctors access to a broad range of knowledge and helps improve patient care.

Temporary Workers Temporary workers work for a short time at a company, but they are hired and paid by independent employment agencies. Temporary workers are used often in health care. If a home health care agency has a sudden increase in clients, for example, a temporary worker might be called in to fill a position.

In health care, temporary workers might serve as medical secretaries or home health care aides. They may fill clerical positions in a hospital or clinic. Hospitals even call in temporary registered nurses to maintain full staffing.

CAREER RESOURCES

GENERAL CAREER RESOURCES

Career Key
www.careerkey.org
A free online self-assessment test that identifies students' Holland career choice personality type.

CTE–Career Technical Education
www.careertech.org/career-clusters/glance/at-a-glance.html
A site featuring definitions and models of career clusters, along with resources about programs of study and real-world examples.

Dictionary of Occupational Titles
www.occupationalinfo.org
A searchable database of job titles and descriptions.

Mapping Your Future
www.mappingyourfuture.org
Career and education planning information for students, from middle school to adult.

Mind Tools
www.mindtools.com
A resource for developing the essential skills and techniques that will help workers excel in any chosen profession.

O*NET
http://online.onetcenter.org
This online resource center offers skills profiles, details about hundreds of individual occupations, and crosswalk to DOT codes.

Occupational Outlook Handbook
www.bls.gov/oco/
The full text of the *Occupational Outlook Handbook* online provides information on education needs, earnings, prospects, descriptions, and conditions of hundreds of jobs.

Salary.com
www.salary.com
A nationwide database of salary information for hundreds of careers.

HEALTH SCIENCE RESOURCES

American Academy of Physician Assistants
www.aapa.org
A national organization representing and supporting physician assistants.

American Dental Association
www.ada.org
A national society that provides oral health information for dentists and their patients.

American Medical Association
www.ama-assn.org
This professional association helps doctors help patients by uniting physicians nationwide to work on important professional and public health issues.

American Physical Therapy Association
www.apta.org
A national professional organization dedicated to fostering advancements in physical therapy.

Centers for Disease Control and Prevention
www.cdc.gov
The federal agency, which is part of the Department of Health and Human Services, protects and promotes health and safety and applies disease prevention and control.

Health Resources and Services Administration
www.hrsa.gov
A branch of the Department of Health and Human Services created to improve and expand access to quality health care.

MedZilla
www.medzilla.com
A career website for workers in biotechnology, pharmaceuticals, health care, and science.

National Center for Assisted Living
www.ncal.org
A branch of the American Health Care Association, dedicated to ensuring quality of care and access to assisted living services.

National Institute for Health Care Management
www.nihcm.org
A nonprofit organization dedicated to improving America's health care system.

PREPARE

This section of *Career Companion: Health Science* provides practice of the skills you will need for any career in health science. It is divided into three workplace skill areas:

READING FOR INFORMATION

LOCATING INFORMATION

APPLIED MATHEMATICS

At the beginning of each section is a list of specific skills presented. Also included are examples of situations in which these skills are likely to be used.

After practicing these workplace skills, you will be able to answer the following questions:

- How can I identify the main idea of a workplace document?
- What do I need to look for when following step-by-step instructions?
- How can workplace graphics help me make decisions?
- What types of calculations do I need to know to do my job?
- How can I solve problems using math operations?

Working your way through each skill area will help you prepare for a job in health science.

READING FOR INFORMATION

Reading for information is a key skill in the health science industry. You may spend your days working in an office, a hospital, or an ambulance. No matter what the job, at some point you will need to read text to gather information. Before applying for a job, you will need to read a job description and understand the duties involved. You may be required to read a job application and understand the information it asks you to provide. Once hired, you may need to read the employee handbook, which lists rules and regulations for your position.

To succeed at a job, you must be able to understand the purpose of texts you encounter and identify the most important ideas and details. You must also know how to respond to them.

In the following pages, you will encounter a variety of workplace documents to read and interpret. You will also use a wide range of reading skills.

When you read a question on the following pages, think about what is being asked and how you might find the answer. Read the text carefully, focusing on the information you are asked to find or the steps you are asked to take. After you have chosen an answer, look back to make sure you have answered the question being asked.

Learning these key reading skills will speed your path to advancement in the health science industry.

KEY SKILLS FOR CAREER SUCCESS

Here are the topics and skills covered in this section and some examples of how you might use them to read different types of materials.

TOPIC	SKILL
Read and Understand Information in Workplace Documents	1. Identify Main Idea and Details 2. Identify Details That Are Not Clearly Stated

Example: As a cardiovascular technician, you may need to find details in a patient's medical file.

Follow Instructions from Workplace Documents	3. Understand and Apply Basic and Multi-Step Instructions 4. Apply Instructions to Unique Situations

Example: As a radiologist, you may need to read instructions to set up and operate a new MRI machine.

Define and Use Words in the Workplace	5. Determine the Meaning of New Words 6. Understand Unique Words and Acronyms 7. Understand and Apply Technical Terms and Jargon

Example: As a medical transcriptionist, you may need to transcribe and edit text that contains medical acronyms, technical terms, and jargon.

Understand and Follow Policies and Procedures in Workplace Documents	8. Apply Workplace Policies and Procedures 9. Understand the Rationale Behind Workplace Policies

Example: As a patient representative, you must understand a medical facility's policies and be able to explain them to a patient.

IDENTIFY MAIN IDEA AND DETAILS

When reading documents such as articles in medical journals or patient files, workers in the health science industry need to be able to identify the main idea. They must also find details supporting the main idea. The main idea tells what the document is about. Details provide more information that helps explain the main idea.

HOPE FOR AN HIV VACCINE

The intervention most anticipated by everyone working to stop the HIV/AIDS epidemic is a vaccine to prevent infection. While some experts working in AIDS research are optimistic, hoping that it can take about 10 years to come up with an AIDS vaccine, let's not forget that it took scientists 42 years to develop a vaccine for whooping cough, 47 years to develop a polio vaccine, and 105 years for a typhoid fever vaccine. While early HIV vaccine trials indicate that the vaccines are not effective in reducing the risk for HIV infection, the trials provided critical information that will guide future research on HIV vaccines.

1. You are a research assistant to an HIV/AIDS researcher working on developing an AIDS vaccine. While studying the work of others who have tried and succeeded to find vaccines for other deadly, life-threatening diseases, you come across an article covering the topic. What is the main idea of the article?

   A. It takes a long time to find a vaccine for a deadly disease.

   B. It took 42 years to develop a vaccine for whooping cough.

   C. It will take a decade to find a vaccine for AIDS.

   D. It took 47 years to find a polio vaccine.

   E. It will take a decade to find a vaccine for HIV/AIDS.

2. Which of the following is a detail that supports the idea that it takes a long time to develop a vaccine for a life-threatening disease?

   A. Typhoid fever is a life-threatening disease.

   B. The most anticipated intervention is a vaccine to prevent infection.

   C. AIDS is an epidemic.

   D. The trials provided information that will guide future research.

   E. It took 105 years to develop a typhoid fever vaccine.

Police Report:

Mr. Jones found his wife dead when he got home from work. He says she was alive when he left for work in the morning. He talked to her on the phone during lunch break but then he lost track of time. He was in meetings until 7 P.M.

He called the police. The police arrived at the scene at 8:15 P.M., when they discovered the body and recorded the legal time of death, later to be submitted to the death certificate office. The ME (medical examiner) estimated the time of death at 1 P.M. The exact time of death may be determined after the ME gets to examine the body in the lab.

3. You work as an assistant to the medical examiner with the police department. Tonight, you receive a phone call from the medical examiner to meet him at a crime scene. He needs your assistance. Usually you take notes on everything he says to later transcribe for him and file it on the computer. From your notes, what is the estimated time of death?

A. 1 p.m.

B. 1:15 p.m.

C. 7 p.m.

D. 8 p.m.

E. 8:15 p.m.

4. What did you write as the legal time of death?

A. 1 p.m.

B. 1:15 p.m.

C. 7 p.m.

D. 8 p.m.

E. 8:15 p.m.

ANSWER KEY

Item 1:   **A** It takes a long time to find a vaccine for a deadly disease.

Item 2:   **E** It took 105 years to develop a typhoid fever vaccine.

Item 3:   **A** 1 p.m.

Item 4:   **E** 8:15 p.m.

IDENTIFY DETAILS THAT ARE NOT CLEARLY STATED

The details in workplace documents are not always clearly stated. For example, a clinical research coordinator may have to base a decision about a person's ability to participate in a clinical study on a variety of information, such as medical records and letters from doctors that do not directly state the person's appropriateness for the study. Details needed to make a decision may be implied, or suggested, rather than stated.

STAFF HANDBOOK VACATION POLICY:

As a staff member at Doctor Daniel Jones, MD, Family Doctor Care, you are entitled to paid leave as follows:

- 10 vacation days and 5 personal days per year, for 1–5 years of employment
- 15 vacation days and 5 personal days per year, for 6–10 years of employment

Vacation requests should be submitted in writing, by e-mail. A 2-week advance notification for vacation is encouraged.

1. You are hired as a nurse at a family doctor's office. According to the Staff Handbook Vacation Policy, how many vacation days can you take after working at the office for 6 months?

    A. 0

    B. 5

    C. 10

    D. 15

    E. 20

2. How should you submit a request for vacation?

    A. through a coworker

    B. by phone

    C. in person

    D. verbally

    E. by e-mail

MEMO:

From: Lab Director

To: Lab Technicians and Tech Assistants

Subject: Blood Sampling Guidelines

- Be sure you don't pose any risk (or only minimum risk) when you draw blood.
- Always ask patients/donors if they want to stretch out on the bed; always allow them to lie down if they request it, so that they don't pass out.
- Never draw more than 550 cc of blood in an 8-week period.
- For adults: draw no more than 200 cc of blood at one time.
- For adults: if you have to draw more than 200 cc at one time, check for the following:
  - weight is at least 110 pounds
  - pulse is between 50 and 100 beats per minute
  - temperature is no more than 99.5°F
  - check for cardiac irregularities
  - ask your head lab technician or nurse if you have any questions.

3. You are a lab technician working at a blood lab that collects blood from donors or research study participants. You receive a memo from the lab director. If a donor gave blood 10 weeks ago, how much blood can you collect today (assuming normal circumstances)?

   A. no more than 50 cc

   B. no more than 100 cc

   C. no more than 110 cc

   D. no more than 200 cc

   E. no more than 550 cc

4. What should you do if the patient weighs less than 110 pounds?

   A. Check that the patient's pulse is 50 to 100 beats per minute.

   B. Check for cardiac irregularities.

   C. Limit the blood draw to a maximum of 200 cc.

   D. Keep the patient's temperature to 99.5°F or less.

   E. Ask if the patient feels dizzy.

ANSWER KEY

Item 1:   **A** 0

Item 2:   **E** by e-mail

Item 3:   **D** no more than 200 cc

Item 4:   **C** Limit the blood draw to a maximum of 200 cc.

Read and
Understand
Information
in Workplace
Documents

**Follow
Instructions
from
Workplace
Documents**

Define and Use
Words in the
Workplace

Understand
and Follow
Policies and
Procedures
in Workplace
Documents

UNDERSTAND AND APPLY BASIC AND MULTI-STEP INSTRUCTIONS

It may be necessary to follow multi-step instructions in a variety of situations, such as when learning a new medical procedure or entering information into a computerized medical record system. Workers must read carefully to know when to take each step, and be able to apply the instructions in a variety of unique situations.

PROCEDURE FOR INSERTING A PICC LINE:

- Disinfect the skin at the bend of the elbow before inserting the PICC line.
- Insert the tubing using the catheter needle and guide it through the patient's vein.
- When the tubing reaches the desired location, closest to the heart, use a dressing to fix the end of the tubing sticking out of the patient's arm.
- Take a chest X-ray to verify that the catheter is in the correct position.
- Begin administering the intravenous medication through the tubing.

1. As a home health aide specialist, you sometimes assist a nurse who is starting or replacing peripheral inserted central catheter lines (or PICC lines), in order to administer intravenous medications. According to the procedure, what will the nurse do when the tubing reaches the desired location?

   A. Start to administer intravenous medication through a PICC line.

   B. Use an X-ray machine to monitor the tubing.

   C. Prepare the intravenous medication administered through the PICC line.

   D. Use a dressing to fix the end of the tubing sticking out of patient's arm.

   E. Disinfect the skin at the bend of the elbow.

2. What is the first thing the nurse does when starting the PICC line?

   A. prepares the medication to be administered through the PICC line

   B. disinfects the PICC line

   C. prepares the X-ray machine used to guide the tubing through the patient's vein

   D. prepares the patient to have the PICC line started

   E. disinfects the skin at the bend of the elbow

PROCEDURE FOR LABELING BLOOD SAMPLE TUBES FOR BLOOD LAB UNIVERSAL:

- Make sure the requisition form has the key elements marked down: patient's name, patient's ID.
- Mark the key elements from the requisition form on the collection tube in this same specific order: patient's surname, first name, and middle initial.
- Mark the other key elements from the requisition form: the patient's ID number; make sure it matches.
- Also mark the date and time and initialize with the phlebotomist's initials (the person who drew the blood) on each of the collection tubes, also the quantity of collection (in milliliters) for each collection tube.
- In case you use an automated system, such as a barcode printer, make sure the same information is correct; the printer will also issue a barcode on the label

3. You are an assistant working in a blood test lab, helping the phlebotomist label the tubes with the blood samples. You follow the procedure. What are the key elements you need to use when labeling the collection tubes?

   A. the patient's date of birth

   B. the patient's name and ID number

   C. the barcode label on each collection tube

   D. the patient's test date

   E. the phlebotomist's initials

4. What is one thing you should mark down on the collection test label?

   A. the collection tube

   B. the barcode

   C. the phlebotomist's initials

   D. the requisition form

   E. the blood sample

ANSWER KEY

Item 1: **D** Use a dressing to fix the end of the tubing sticking out of patient's arm.

Item 2: **E** disinfects the skin at the bend of the elbow

Item 3: **B** the patient's name and ID number

Item 4: **C** the phlebotomist's initials

SKILL

4

Read and
Understand
Information
in Workplace
Documents

Follow
Instructions
from
Workplace
Documents

Define and Use
Words in the
Workplace

Understand
and Follow
Policies and
Procedures
in Workplace
Documents

APPLY INSTRUCTIONS TO UNIQUE SITUATIONS

A set of instructions may call for different actions in different situations. For example, a home health aide may need to understand and apply a doctor's instructions in different ways when caring for several patients. Home health aides are not closely supervised by a doctor, so they must be able to apply general instructions to a variety of situations.

PROCEDURE FOR CLEANING UP BLOOD SPILLS AND BLOOD-CONTAMINATED MATERIAL:

1. Check personal protective equipment (PPE) for tears and damages before wearing. Use of gloves is mandatory; face mask is required if the cleanup of blood is above chest level and/or when splashing may occur; use disposable coverall when blood splashing may occur; booties are required when walking on blood-contaminated surfaces.

2. Clean contaminated blood surfaces using absorbent powder or pad on blood until completely absorbed. Only then remove the pad using gloves and place it in the garbage bag. Use scoop to remove powder and place it in garbage bag.

3. Use an EPA-registered disinfectant spray (bleach or hydrogen peroxide) on contaminated areas; leave spray on for 7 minutes; mop with reusable mop if surface is wood; use extraction device if surface is carpet or furniture; disinfect and decontaminate any reusable equipment by soaking it in bucket of disinfectant solution, then dump waste water down sanitary drain.

4. Finishing cleanup: place all disposable cleanup material in garbage bag; then remove PPE with caution (gloves last) and place it in doubled garbage bag. Wash hands and notify your supervisor.

1. As a hospital custodian, you have been specially trained to clean up blood spills and materials contaminated by blood. According to the procedures, what do you do if the PPE is damaged?

   A. Use the part that's not damaged.

   B. Use it as is, but be extra careful.

   C. Report to the supervisor.

   D. Replace it with a new one.

   E. Repair it as best you can before using.

2. According to the procedures, what do you use to decontaminate a wooden floor?

   A. bucket of disinfectant solution

   B. tongs or dust pan

   C. rigid sealable containers

   D. absorbent powder or pad

   E. disinfectant spray and mop

MEMO TO MEDICAL OFFICE ASSISTANTS:

New Patient Appointment Procedures:

- Ask the patient which doctor he or she would like to see.
- Ask for the preferred appointment date and verify in the scheduling software that date/time is available with the doctor; if the desired time is not available, suggest different times when the doctor is available.
- Enter the patient's name and select the time and doctor's name using the scheduling software.
- Confirm the appointment time, date, and doctor.
- Inform the patient of the cancellation policy: cancellations within 24 hours will result in the patient being charged a cancellation fee.
- If a patient later cancels or reschedules an appointment, reschedule the appointment using the scheduling software and confirm the new date. If the patient cancels or reschedules an appointment within 24 hours of the original appointment, inform the patient that a cancellation fee will apply.

3. You are a new assistant at a multi-doctor office. Your supervisor explains the office rules and hands you the memo with instructions on how to handle first time patients. What should you do if the patient's preferred appointment time is not available?

A. Type in the patient's name and doctor's name in the software.

B. Offer alternative times when the preferred doctor is available.

C. Schedule the appointment when the doctor is available.

D. Confirm the appointment date, time, and patient's name.

E. Select a different doctor.

4. When must you charge the patient a cancellation fee?

A. if the patient calls to reschedule an appointment 48 hours before the original appointment

B. if the patient calls to cancel an appointment 48 hours before the original appointment

C. if the patient calls to reschedule an appointment a week before the original appointment

D. if the patient calls to reschedule an appointment the day of the appointment

E. if the patient calls to cancel an appointment 36 hours before the original appointment

ANSWER KEY

Item 1:   **D** Replace it with a new one.
Item 2:   **E** disinfectant spray and mop
Item 3:   **B** Offer alternative times when the preferred doctor is available.
Item 4:   **D** if the patient calls to reschedule an appointment the day of the appointment

Read and
Understand
Information
in Workplace
Documents

Follow
Instructions
from Workplace
Documents

**Define and
Use Words in
the Workplace**

Understand
and Follow
Policies and
Procedures
in Workplace
Documents

DETERMINE THE MEANING OF NEW WORDS

Health science workers occasionally come across words whose meaning is unclear. Some may be defined in the text, while others require the reader to discover the meaning. For example, a medical transcriptionist might come across an unfamiliar medical term when reviewing the transcript of a doctor's dictation. The context surrounding the word and the reader's background knowledge can help clarify the word's meaning.

TAKING TEMPERATURE USING THERMOMETERS

Thermometers are used to take temperatures from many different locations. For example, oral temperatures may be taken only with a sub-lingual thermometer placed under the tongue. A tympanic thermometer measures the temperature of the tympanum, or eardrum. A band thermometer is applied to the patient's brow, or forehead.

1. As a health aide at a local clinic, you need to know how and when to use different types of thermometers. Where is a **sub-lingual** thermometer placed?

   A. under the tongue

   B. on the brow

   C. in the mouth

   D. over the tongue

   E. in the ear

2. What does the term **tympanum** mean?

   A. tongue

   B. mouth

   C. eardrum

   D. forehead

   E. brow

USING BED RESTRAINTS TO PREVENT FALLS

Falls are common for patients, especially older ones. Patients can become dizzy, confused, or unconscious because of hearing or vision problems, medication they are taking, or other illnesses.

Only doctors should decide if a patient needs bed restraints. Part of your job as a nurse assistant is to prevent patients from harming themselves due to falls. One way of doing that is by using bed restraints, called side rails or bed rails.

Side rails are located on each side of the patient's bed; they can be raised or lowered as needed to prevent the patient from falling from the bed; the nurse assistant can lock them into place. Alert patients, who are aware of their surroundings, may consider themselves confined or even embarrassed to have the side bed rails raised; in this situation ask your supervisor for advice.

3. You are a nurse assistant in a nursing home. In your procedures manual, you find instruction on how to keep patients safe by using bed restraints. What do **bed restraints** do?

    A. keep patients comfortable while they sleep

    B. keep patients from becoming dizzy or confused

    C. prevent patients from falling out of bed

    D. help avoid embarrassment to the patient

    E. keep patients confined

4. What does **alert** mean?

    A. confused

    B. aware

    C. present

    D. awake

    E. able

ANSWER KEY

Item 1:   **A** under the tongue

Item 2:   **C** eardrum

Item 3:   **C** prevent patients from falling out of bed

Item 4:   **B** aware

UNDERSTAND UNIQUE WORDS AND ACRONYMS

Acronyms (words made from the initials of several words) and unique terms may sometimes be used without explanation in work situations. For example, a medical office assistant may need to understand common acronyms and abbreviations for medical tests, such as a CAT (computerized axial tomography) scan, in order to help schedule a patient's tests. To understand these terms, readers should use prior knowledge and study the context, or the information surrounding the words.

KINESIOLOGY: HOW TO USE THE SCIENCE OF HUMAN MOVEMENT TO IMPROVE OUR POSTURE AND LIFE

Kinesiology, or human kinetics, is the science of human movement and the body posture during movement. Applied kinesiology is used by many practitioners (including chiropractors, osteopaths, medical doctors, and dentists) to evaluate body functions by using different muscle tests. Applied kinesiology practitioners ask patients to perform muscle tests, to better examine structural factors such as posture and gait. Then practitioners apply light fingertip massage to pressure points on the body and/or head, to stimulate or relax key muscles. Because it works on tissues that are connected, kinesiology is used to improve a patient's digestion, energy, joint pain, allergies, asthma, and headaches.

1. You are a holistic medicine practitioner who wants to specialize in applied kinesiology. When you study for an upcoming practical test, you come across this article excerpt. What does the phrase **pressure points** mean in the context of this article?

   A. areas of pain caused by too much stress at work

   B. relaxed points on the body

   C. points on the skin on which practitioners apply force

   D. structural factors such as posture and gait

   E. pain in the joints caused by allergies or asthma

2. What is the meaning of **kinetics** in this excerpt?

   A. massage of key parts of the body

   B. stimulation of key muscles

   C. transfer of energy between tissues

   D. movement of the human body

   E. the practice of kinesiology

CALL FOR VOLUNTEERS

The Department of Children Services (DCS) is looking for volunteers to help children and youth in the community. Volunteers must be at least 18 years of age. The DCS is looking for volunteers from different social-economic and educational backgrounds who will be a positive influence on and supportive of children and youth. They must also have the skills and qualities needed to be an effective volunteer.

Volunteers must live in the state. Non-residents cannot volunteer with the Department of Children's Services unless special permission is obtained from the District Office (DO) where the individual wants to volunteer. The head of the DCS must approve any decisions the DO makes regarding out-of-state volunteers.

3. As a recently hired volunteer coordinator in human services, you have received this qualifications document. According to the document, the DCS must sanction approval for out-of-state volunteers. What do the letters DCS stand for?

    A. Drug Counseling for Students

    B. Direct Counseling and Services

    C. Department of Care for Suffering

    D. Development for Children Services

    E. Department of Children's Services

4. What do the letters DO stand for in the second paragraph?

    A. District Office

    B. Department Officer

    C. Dedicated Opportunity

    D. Direct Occupation

    E. Director of Operations

ANSWER KEY

Item 1:   **C** points on the skin on which practitioners apply force

Item 2:   **D** movement of the human body

Item 3:   **E** Department of Children's Services

Item 4:   **A** District Office

UNDERSTAND AND APPLY TECHNICAL TERMS AND JARGON

Some workplace documents use technical terms and jargon that are specific to the health science industry. Optometrists may need to understand technical terms relating to vision problems in order to learn about new procedures for correcting vision, for example. They must be able to interpret the meanings of these terms and apply them to the situation at hand.

RADIOLOGIC EXAMINATIONS USING CONTRAST MEDIA

Certain materials or gases can be injected into veins, arteries, lymphatics, or hollow cavities to obtain contrast with the surrounding tissues. A contrast medium is a radiopaque substance which obstructs the passage of X-rays so that the structures containing it appear white on the X-ray film, thus delineating abnormal pouches or growths and defining the contour of body structures on X-ray. Examples of radiopaque material are Hypaque and Renografin, dyes used in intravenous pyelogram (IVP) and barium (the substance used in gastrointestinal series).

1. You are a new radiology technician reviewing training materials for certification. In the simplest terms, what does a **contrast medium** do?

   A. detects materials or gases

   B. treats gastrointestinal diseases

   C. treats abnormal growths

   D. detects radiopaque materials

   E. defines contours of internal body structures

2. A **radiopaque** substance has the ability to do what?

   A. enhance visible light

   B. block visible light

   C. enhance X-rays

   D. block X-rays

   E. protect someone from radiation damage

CARPAL TUNNEL SYNDROME TREATMENTS MANUAL FOR OCCUPATIONAL THERAPISTS

Carpal Tunnel Syndrome, or CTS, is caused by repetitive motion of the hand/wrist. CTS occurs when the patient puts stress on the nerve that runs through a sheath in the wrist to the fingers, or the carpal tunnel, causing tingling, sometimes even numbness, weakening of the hand and fingers, and inability to handle small, detailed objects or to squeeze the hand shut.

Treatment involves therapy, cortisone shots in the affected wrist or, if nothing else works, surgery. During the surgery, a hand surgeon makes a 2-inch incision through which the surgeon then cuts the carpal tunnel ligament, thus enlarging the carpal tunnel.

Occupational therapist (OT) assistants specialized in treating carpal tunnel syndrome (CTS) can care for their patients in several ways. The OT assistant can recommend and advise on ergonomic equipment that the patient can use at work to avoid tension in the affected wrist and prevent developing CTS in the good wrist. The use of ergonomically designed equipment helps keep the body in a natural position which, in turn, prevents stress and damage.

3. You are an occupational therapist and are reading an article on treatment for carpel tunnel syndrome. What is the **carpal tunnel**?

   A. a ligament in the fingers

   B. tingling or numbness in the wrist

   C. a nerve sheath in the wrist

   D. weakening of the hands and fingers

   E. bones in the wrist

4. What does **ergonomic** design mean?

   A. allows for repetitive motion

   B. causes tingling or numbness in the hands and fingers

   C. keeps the body stressed while at the computer

   D. supports the body in a natural position

   E. puts stress on the nerve in the wrist

ANSWER KEY

Item 1: **E** defines contours of internal body structures

Item 2: **D** block X-rays

Item 3: **C** a nerve sheath in the wrist

Item 4: **D** supports the body in a natural position

APPLY WORKPLACE POLICIES AND PROCEDURES

Most health science workers receive a policies and procedures manual when they begin work. It is important not just to understand the text of the manual, but to also apply the policies to their actual work situation. For example, understanding the principles behind a hospital's policy on employee immunizations helps workers comply with the policy and prevent the spread of contagious diseases.

HR POLICY FOR HOME HEALTH WORKERS

- The home health aide has 2 weeks paid vacation and 5 personal days if employed between 0 and 3 years; the number of vacation days increases gradually (add 1 day) with each additional year
- Punctuality is important
- Employees who are late for work (15 minutes or more) 3 consecutive days without prior notice will be given a verbal warning
- Employees who continue to be late for work after receiving a verbal warning will be given a written warning
- Employees who continue this kind of behavior will be fired
- This procedure also applies to aides who miss work without excuse
- Similar rules apply if the supervisor receives patient complaints regarding an employee

1. You are a supervisor working with home health aides. You are explaining the HR policy to a new hire. What is the principle behind this policy?

   A. Tardiness is not an important issue.

   B. Aides should take personal days.

   C. Employees should not be late when visiting with a patient.

   D. Employees should take vacation time.

   E. Employees should manage their time well.

2. Why is this policy important to the home health aide company?

   A. to ensure that the employee understands how to do the job

   B. to ensure that the employee understands the contract

   C. to ensure that the employee is dependable

   D. to ensure that the employee knows his or her rights to paid vacation

   E. to ensure that the employee is ready to start work

APPOINTMENT REMINDER E-MAIL PROCEDURES

Be sure to send two e-mails to all patients to remind them of an upcoming appointment. Send one e-mail 3 weeks before the appointment and another 3 days before the appointment. For new patients only, the e-mails MUST explain the cancellation policy. Be sure to explain that patients will be charged a $75 cancellation fee if they do not give at least 24 hours notice before canceling or do not show up for their scheduled appointment. The cancellation policy reminder is not necessary for established patients.

Like any other form of communication with our clients, e-mails should be professional in tone and content. Keep the writing style clear and concise. Keep sentences short. Always proofread for grammar and typos before sending. Do not write in ALL CAPS, unless it is something extremely important and you explain the reason for your all caps in a note at the bottom of your e-mail. Be as polite and courteous in an e-mail as you'd be face-to-face or in print.

3. You are one of three office managers working in a medical group. Your job is to keep track of patients' appointments and remind them of their scheduled appointments. You receive a memo from the group director. What is the main purpose of the memo?

A. to make sure the staff provide necessary information to patients in a professional way

B. to maintain professionalism when corresponding with other businesses

C. to remind office staff of the need to write clearly and concisely in all office communications

D. to increase patient satisfaction

E. to use e-mail communication to attract new clients

4. Which one of the following is not necessary when writing to established patients?

A. communicating their scheduled appointment time and day

B. explaining the cancellation charge

C. following the "ALL CAPS" rule

D. proofreading for grammar and typos

E. maintaining a professional tone

ANSWER KEY

Item 1: **E** Employees should manage their time well.
Item 2: **C** to ensure that the employee is dependable
Item 3: **A** to make sure the staff provide necessary information to patients in a professional way
Item 4: **B** explaining the cancellation charge

9

UNDERSTAND THE RATIONALE BEHIND WORKPLACE POLICIES

As with any industry, workplace policies in the health science industry are created for a reason. When interacting with a hospital patient, it is helpful for staff members to understand the reasoning behind hospital policies on acceptable contact with patients. This knowledge helps the staff ensure that policies meant to protect patients and staff are being followed correctly.

PROCEDURE FOR SURVEY ON MIGRAINE PATIENTS

In an effort to continue to develop new medications for migraine sufferers, we are designing a survey that would give us more insights into patient-medical therapy interaction. The information they give us will be instrumental in developing new drugs to help migraine sufferers.

In order to select the right participants, do the following:

- Send an e-mail questionnaire to our subscribers; questions should identify migraine sufferers, what kind of medications they take, what side effects they experience, if they are willing to try a new medication
- Call those who qualify for the next step, to very their e-mail answers
- Inform participants who qualify for the next step about the time, place, duration and payment for the survey
- At the survey facility, upon participants' arrival, confirm participant names, and send them to the room where the survey takes place

1. As a clinical research scientist, you must follow your company's procedure for the selection of survey participants. What is the rationale behind these procedures?

   A. to help migraine sufferers with their migraine pain

   B. to offer medications to migraine sufferers

   C. to run the surveys efficiently

   D. to ensure that the right participants are selected

   E. to ensure that new migraine medication will be developed

2. Why is it important to select appropriate participants?

   A. to obtain detailed information about new migraine medications

   B. to move forward in developing new migraine medications

   C. to assist the participants in choosing migraine medications

   D. to obtain client contact information for marketing purposes

   E. to obtain information to better understand migraine medication interaction

DRUG LOTTERY GUIDELINES

- As part of the expanded access program (EAP), we have decided to release our new Big Drug to patients. It has passed level 3 testing and awaits FDA approval, but many patients need it now. We will be able to offer our new drug only to a specified number of at-risk patients who will be chosen by lottery. To enter the lottery and have a chance to participate in EAP, patients must meet specific requirements:
- Patient is in stage 4 cancer
- Patient age is 60 years or older
- Patient should have with him/her a complete list of blood test results, as recent as a month prior to the date of applying for this survey
- Patient has tried chemotherapy or radiation at least 5 times
- Patient has had cancer-related surgery
- Patient should have blood test results to prove he/she in stage 4
- Patient should not be in remission

3. You are a clinical research coordinator working with a drug testing team at a pharmaceutical company. You have been asked to coordinate the lottery selection of the patients who will be able to receive the new drug. What is the rationale behind this lottery?

   A. to help at-risk patients who have run out of currently FDA-approved options

   B. to develop new cancer medications that will help lottery participants

   C. to bypass the process of FDA approval for cancer medications

   D. to continue the FDA drug approval procedure and release the drug to the general public

   E. to help patients who are older than 50 and who are currently in stage 3

4. What is the purpose of the strict entry requirements?

   A. to ensure a scientifically valid study

   B. to ensure only those patients who are most at risk receive the drug

   C. because of the cost of the drug

   D. to comply with FDA regulations

   E. to prevent abuse of the drug

ANSWER KEY

Item 1:   **D** to ensure that the right participants are selected

Item 2:   **E** to obtain information to better understand migraine medication interaction

Item 3:   **A** to help at-risk patients who have run out of currently FDA-approved options

Item 4:   **B** to ensure only those patients who are most at risk receive the drug

SKILLS PRACTICE

LOCATING INFORMATION

To succeed in a health science career, you must be able to effectively locate information. Information comes in a variety of forms, including tables, graphs, maps, and diagrams. You may need to locate this information in a graphic on a computer screen, in a document, or even posted on a bulletin board or wall.

Locating information means more than just finding it. It also means understanding it and making use of it in the job you do each day. It may also mean finding missing information and adding it to a graphic.

In the following pages, you will encounter a variety of workplace documents. You will be asked to find important information in these documents. In some cases you must interpret information in these documents. For example, you may need to compare data, summarize data, or sort through distracting information.

When you read a question on the following pages, think about what is being asked and how you might find the answer. Look carefully at the graphic, focusing on the information you are asked to find or the steps you are asked to take. After you have chosen an answer, look back to make sure you have answered the question being asked.

Learning these key locating information skills will speed your path to advancement in the health science industry.

KEY SKILLS FOR CAREER SUCCESS

Here are the topics and skills covered in this section and some examples of how you might use them to locate information in different types of graphics.

TOPIC	SKILL
Locate and Compare Information in Graphics	1. Find Information in Workplace Graphics 2. Enter Information into Workplace Graphics

Example: As a clinical data manager, you may need to review or create charts from information gathered in clinical trials.

Analyze Trends in Workplace Graphics	3. Identify Trends in Workplace Graphics 4. Compare Trends in Workplace Graphics

Example: As an informatics nurse specialist, you may need to find trends in graphs representing nursing data.

Use Information from Workplace Graphics	5. Summarize Information in Workplace Graphics 6. Make Decisions Based on Workplace Graphics

Example: As a substance abuse social worker, you may need to review checklists that compare treatment options and help patients make plans based on that information.

**Locate and
Compare
Information
in Graphics**

Analyze Trends
in Workplace
Graphics

Use Information
from Workplace
Graphics

FIND INFORMATION IN WORKPLACE GRAPHICS

When reading a workplace graphic such as a patient's medical record, health science workers must know what information to look for. The key information may be in one or more documents. Workers must be able to sift through irrelevant or distracting information to find what is needed.

AIDS-Associated Infections

Opportunistic Infections (OI)	Type of Infection	Affected Areas
Candidiasis	Fungus called Candida albicans	appears as white spots in the mouth
Kaposi's sarcoma (KS)	Cancer attacking the capillary linings of organs like skin and internal organs	on the skin it looks like purple blotches
Pneumocystis carinii pneumonia (PCP)	Caused by a parasite called Pneumocystis carinii	it affects only the lungs
Cytomegalovirus (CMV)	A herpes virus	affects primarily the retina, but also the lungs and the digestive system
Mycobacterium avium-intracellulare (MAI)	Caused by a bacterium found in soil and water	Systemic infection with fever, diarrhea, lung and blood disease, and wasting

1. You are a nurse assistant in the AIDS ward of a local hospital. To better prepare for both your patients and for your upcoming certification exams, you study the opportunistic infections (OI) associated with AIDS. They are listed in the table. Which OI affects only the lungs?

   A. candidiasis

   B. Kaposi's sarcoma (KS)

   C. pneumocystis carinii pneumonia (PCP)

   D. cytomegalovirus (CMV)

   E. mycobacterium avium-intracellulare (MAI)

2. Which opportunistic infection appears as purplish blotches on the skin?

   A. Kaposi's sarcoma

   B. candidiasis

   C. pneumocystis carinii pneumonia (PCP)

   D. cytomegalovirus (CMV)

   E. mycobacterium avium-intracellulare (MAI)

Prescription Form:

Doctor John Smith, M.D.
Family Medicine
23 Street, Township City
(tel): 555-222-3343

Patient Name: Emile Jones

Date: 2/12/11

Tests requested: lipid profile (HDL, LDL, cholesterol
total, cholesterol ratio, triglycerides)
Glucose
PSA
CBC (WBC, RBC, urinalyses)

Signature: John Smith M.D.

Lab Facility Information Form:

Medical Lab
456 Main Street, Township City
(tel): 555-333-4566

Hours: 7.30 AM - 4 PM, M-F

All Insurances Accepted

3. You are a nurse and your job is to make sure your patients understand the next steps they must take before they leave the doctor's office. Your patient has two forms in his hand: one is a prescription form with the blood tests he is required to have performed, and the other is a form with information regarding the blood test laboratory. What's the name of the facility where the patient must go for his blood tests?

A. Medical Lab

B. Dr. John Smith

C. Township City

D. 456 Main Street

E. Family Medicine

4. The doctor requests a series of tests based on the patient's exam. What are two of the lipid tests he has requested?

A. HDL, RBC

B. triglycerides, LDL

C. HDL, glucose

D. urinalyses, WBC

E. LDL, PSA

ANSWER KEY

Item 1: **C** pneumocystis carinii pneumonia (PCP)

Item 2: **A** Kaposi's sarcoma

Item 3: **A** Medical Lab

Item 4: **B** triglycerides, LDL

ENTER INFORMATION INTO WORKPLACE GRAPHICS

It may be necessary at times to add information to graphics as part of a job in health science. As a home health aide or nurse, you may need to enter a patient's blood pressure, blood sugar, or other information into a chart or graph. Knowing how to correctly add this information is an important skill in this industry.

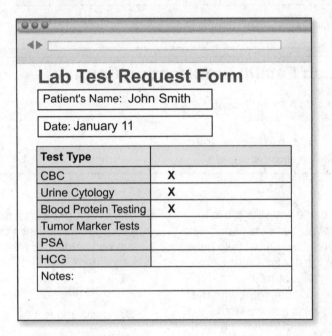

1. As a medical lab technician, you fill out the test request forms. The doctor has requested a PSA test be performed to check for prostate cancer. How do you indicate this test on the test request form?

    A. type "Check for prostate cancer" in the Notes section

    B. enter an "X" in the box next to "PSA"

    C. type "Check for cancer" in the Notes section

    D. enter an "X" in the box next to "Tumor Marker Tests"

    E. enter an "X" in the box next to "HCG"

2. Before you send John Smith's blood sample out for testing, his doctor calls to says that he does not need the blood protein test after all. How do you indicate this change in the request form?

    A. type "No blood protein testing" in the Notes section

    B. remove the "X" for the Blood Protein Testing

    C. start with a new request form

    D. type a note saying "Test for blood protein"

    E. remove the "X" next to CBC

Measures and Data Sources for Environmental Public Health Indicators for Lead

Indicator	Suggested Measure	Potential Data Source
Hazards		
Lead contamination in the environment *(optional)*	1) Proportion of housing stock built before 1950 (optional) 2) Lead levels in sediment and in game or commercial fish (optional)	**CB** **HUD** **States of local jurisdiction:** environmental protection agencies, especially those with indicator projects.
Residence near metal processing industries *(developmental)*	1) Proportion of population residing near lead smelters (developmental)	**CB** **HUD**
Exposure		
Blood lead level (in children) *(core)*	1) Proportion of high-risk children with elevated blood lead level (core)	**CDC: NHAMCS**; Lead Surveillance Program **States or local jurisdictions:** prevalence surveys
Health Effect		
Lead posioning (in children) *(core)*	1) Number of hospitalizations from lead poisoning in children (core)	**CDC:** NHAMCS; NHDS **States or local jurisdictions:** hospital discharge surveys
Intervention		
Lead elimination programs *(optional)*	1) Number of jurisdictions with lead training and certification programs (optional) 2) Proportion of population living in pre-1950 housing that has been tested for the presence of lead-based paint (optional) 3) Number of completed lead abatements (developmental)	**CB** **CDC:** NHIS **EPA** **HUD** **States or local jurisdictions** **Private sector:** industry monitoring systems

3. You are an environmental epidemiologist working for a local public health department. You are reviewing a federal publication on environmental public health indicators for various factors, including lead. According to the chart, what indicator do you use to verify lead exposure?

   A. lead contamination in the environment

   B. proximity to metal processing facilities

   C. lead poisoning in children

   D. blood lead level in children

   E. lead elimination programs

4. According to the chart, what is the suggested measurement of the health effects of lead poisoning?

   A. the proportion of housing built before 1950

   B. the proportion of high-risk children with elevated blood lead levels

   C. the number of hospitalizations due to lead poisoning in children

   D. the number of jurisdictions with lead training and certification programs

   E. lead levels in sediment or fish

ANSWER KEY

Item 1: **B** enter an "X" in the box next to "PSA"

Item 2: **B** remove the "X" for the Blood Protein Testing

Item 3: **D** blood lead level in children

Item 4: **C** the number of hospitalizations due to lead poisoning in children

IDENTIFY TRENDS IN WORKPLACE GRAPHICS

Health science workers must sometimes analyze graphics to identify trends. They might search for data that has increased or decreased over time. A physician's assistant might study graphics to find trends in patients' lab results. A clinical data manager might look for trends in clinical trial data. Being able to identify common trends from graphics can help with a variety of jobs in this industry.

Estimated rate* of human immunodeficiency virus/acquired immunodeficiency syndrome (HIV/AIDS) diagnosis, by race/ethnicity and year of diagnosis—33 states, 2001–2004

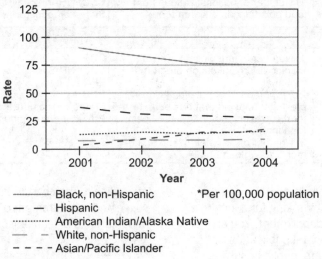

——— Black, non-Hispanic   *Per 100,000 population
— — Hispanic
············ American Indian/Alaska Native
— — White, non-Hispanic
— — — Asian/Pacific Islander

1. As an HIV educator, you teach classes at a local community college. You present statistics on HIV/AIDS diagnoses by race or ethnicity. What trend do you observe in this graph?

   A. All races show a decline in HIV/AIDS diagnoses since 2001.

   B. HIV/AIDS diagnoses in Hispanics have increased since 2001.

   C. HIV/AIDS diagnoses in Blacks and Hispanics have decreased since 2001.

   D. HIV/AIDS diagnoses in American Indians have decreased since 2001.

   E. HIV/AIDS diagnoses in Whites have decreased since 2001.

2. Which race or ethnicity has experienced the greatest increase in HIV/AIDS diagnoses since 2001?

   A. Black, non-Hispanic

   B. Hispanic

   C. American Indian/Alaska Native

   D. White, non-Hispanic

   E. Asian/Pacific Islander

Estimated Number of Serious Sports Injuries Among Persons 35–54 Years of Age, Associated with 16 Popular Sports Categories, 1991 and 1998

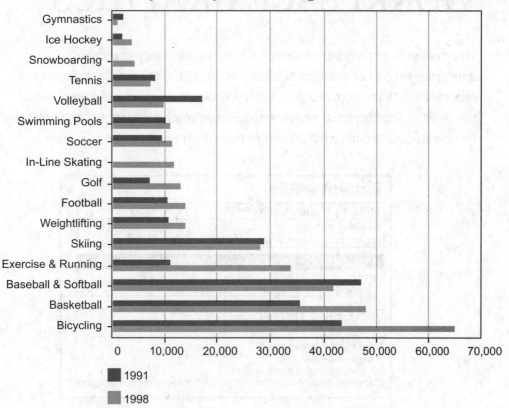

3. As a sports clinical specialist in an injury rehabilitation center, you treat sports injuries in people of all ages, including "baby boomers" (people born between 1946 and 1964). Which of the following lists includes only sports that showed an increase in serious sports injuries from 1991 to 1998?

A. tennis, skiing, golf

B. soccer, running, basketball

C. volleyball, football, baseball

D. gymnastics, skiing, softball

E. tennis, baseball, softball

4. Which of the following lists includes sports that had at least 20,000 serious injuries in 1998?

A. gymnastics, ice hockey, skiing

B. tennis, weightlifting, golf

C. running, basketball, bicycling

D. tennis, soccer, softball

E. in-line skating, golf, basketball

ANSWER KEY

Item 1: **C** HIV/AIDS diagnoses in Blacks and Hispanics have decreased since 2001.

Item 2: **E** Asian/Pacific Islander

Item 3: **B** soccer, running, basketball

Item 4: **C** running, basketball, bicycling

Locate and
Compare
Information
in Graphics

**Analyze
Trends in
Workplace
Graphics**

Use Information
from Workplace
Graphics

COMPARE TRENDS IN WORKPLACE GRAPHICS

When reviewing workplace graphics, it may be necessary to compare information in one or more graphics. A pathologist might compare maps of reported infections from different years to track the patterns of the spread of the disease. Workers must know how different graphics relate to each other, and be able to compare information and trends within them.

Patient's File:

Patient's Name: Joanna Phillip			**DOB:** 1970
Hygiene notes: patient has problems with gingivitis			

1/25/2010	5/20/2010	9/27/2010	*1/19/2011*
X-rays			
Cleaning	Cleaning	Cleaning	
Checkup		Checkup	
Root canal	New Crown		
Bridge work			

Treatment frequency:
X-rays: once per year
Checkup: every 6 months
Cleaning: every 6 months (4 months for patients with gingivitis)

Appointments

Your next scheduled visit is with (Dentist):
_____

On (day, date): _____

At (time): _____
Call at least 24-hours in advance with
cancelations and changes to appointments.
(345) 555-1234

---

1. You are a dental hygienist. Your job is to make sure patients are scheduled for regular checkups and other appointments. You have just finished Joanna's September 2010 cleaning. Which treatments should you schedule for Joanna in January 2011?

   A. cleaning only

   B. cleaning and checkup

   C. X-rays only

   D. cleaning, X-rays, and root canal

   E. cleaning and X-rays

2. After Joanna's September 2010 visit, you fill out an appointment card. What do you write on her appointment card as the date of her next scheduled appointment?

   A. 1/25/2010

   B. 05/20/2010

   C. 09/27/2011

   D. 01/19/2011

   E. 05/18/2011

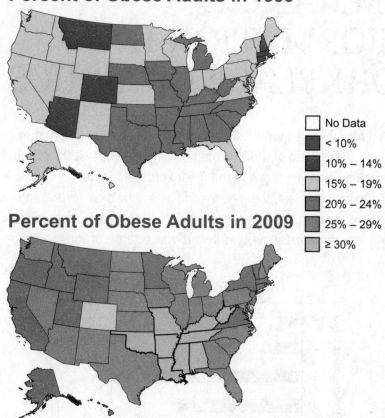

Percent of Obese Adults in 1999

Percent of Obese Adults in 2009

Legend:
- No Data
- < 10%
- 10% – 14%
- 15% – 19%
- 20% – 24%
- 25% – 29%
- ≥ 30%

3. You are a nutritionist working at a weight clinic for severely obese patients. According to the maps for 1999 and 2009, what national trend do you see?

A. Obesity rates have increased in most US states.

B. Obesity rates have increased in every US state.

C. Obesity rates have remained about the same.

D. Obesity rates have decreased in most US states.

E. Obesity rates have decreased in every US state.

4. Which statement best describes the obesity rates in the United States in 2009?

A. Obesity rates are 10 percent or higher in every state but one.

B. Obesity rates are 15 percent or higher in every state but one.

C. Obesity rates are 20 percent or higher in every state but one.

D. Obesity rates are 25 percent or higher in every state but one.

E. Obesity rates are 30 percent or higher in every state but one.

ANSWER KEY

Item 1: **E** cleaning and X-rays
Item 2: **D** 01/19/2011
Item 3: **B** Obesity rates have increased in every U.S. state.
Item 4: **C** Obesity rates are 20 percent or higher in every state but one.

SUMMARIZE INFORMATION IN WORKPLACE GRAPHICS

When workers look at a graphic such as a diagram or a bar graph, they need to analyze and make sense of the information. It may be necessary to summarize the information, or boil it down to the most important facts. For example, a school dietitian might review the Nutrition Facts panels on several cafeteria foods to keep the total saturated fat of school lunches within an acceptable range. Being able to summarize allows workers to make sense of varying information.

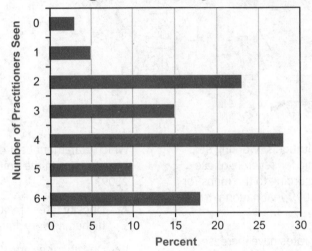

Migraine Survey Results

1. As a medical office manager working in a neurologist's office, you administer surveys to new patients. How could you summarize the results of the migraine survey?

   A. Migraine sufferers do not generally consult specialists.

   B. Many people suffer from migraines.

   C. Most migraine sufferers consult very few specialists.

   D. Most migraine sufferers consult only one specialist.

   E. Most migraine sufferers consult more than one specialist.

2. How many practitioners does the greatest percentage of migraine sufferers see?

   A. 2

   B. 3

   C. 4

   D. 5

   E. over 6

Placement of Peripherally Inserted Central Catheter (PICC)

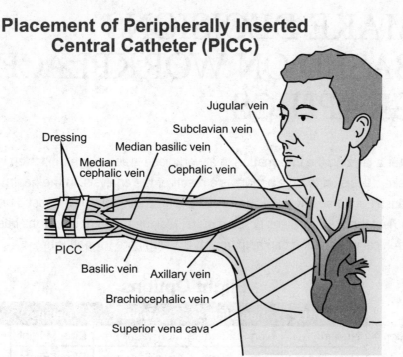

Jugular vein

Subclavian vein

Dressing

Median basilic vein

Median cephalic vein

Cephalic vein

PICC

Basilic vein

Axillary vein

Brachiocephalic vein

Superior vena cava

3. You are a nurse reviewing the method for inserting peripherally inserted central catheter (PICC) lines. PICC lines are used in cancer patients' arms to administer medications and/or nutrients intravenously. You insert the PICC line tubing (catheter) into the vein at the bend of patient's arm and then guide it until it is near the heart. What holds the PICC line in place?

    A. the catheter

    B. tubing

    C. dressing

    D. arm muscles

    E. the patient

4. According to the illustration, in which vein does the PICC line end?

    A. cephalic vein

    B. superior vena cava

    C. basilic vein

    D. subclavia vein

    E. jugular vein

ANSWER KEY

Item 1: **E** Most migraine sufferers consult more than one specialist.

Item 2: **C** 4

Item 3: **C** dressing

Item 4: **B** superior vena cava

MAKE DECISIONS BASED ON WORKPLACE GRAPHICS

Locate and Compare Information in Graphics

Analyze Trends in Workplace Graphics

Use Information from Workplace Graphics

After analyzing the information in a workplace graphic, the next step is often to make a decision or take action as a result of the analysis. In the health science industry, a nurse might decide to call the attending physician based on records of the patient's vital signs or lab results. Making the right decisions based on graphical information can help improve health care for patients.

Flight Options

	Airport	Departure	Arrival	Details	Price
Option 1	Newark	Mon 9:20 am	Mon 12:10 pm	Direct Flight	$320 round trip
	New Orleans	Tues 3:20 pm	Tues 6:50 pm	Direct Flight	
Option 2	Newark	Mon 5:30 pm	Mon 8:50 pm	Direct Flight	$270 round trip
	New Orleans	Tues 2:35 pm	Tues 5:40 pm	Direct Flight	
Option 3	Newark	Mon 2:30 pm	Mon 5:50 pm	Direct Flight	$195 round trip
	New Orleans	Tues 1:35 pm	Tues 4:40 pm	Direct Flight	
Option 4	Newark	Mon 2:30 pm	Mon 5:50 pm	Direct Flight	$185 round trip
	New Orleans	Tues 3:35 pm	Tues 6:40 pm	Direct Flight	
Option 5	Newark	Mon 9:00 pm	Mon 11:30 pm	Direct Flight	$175 round trip
	New Orleans	Tues 1:35 pm	Tues 4:40 pm	Direct Flight	

1. You are a massage therapist in Newark, NJ. Next Monday you have to fly to New Orleans for a shiatsu massage workshop held the following Tuesday morning. Your criteria for choosing a flight are, in order of priority: 1) returning to Newark as soon as possible on Tuesday; 2) having time for dinner in New Orleans; and 3) a low price. What is the best option?

   A. Option 1

   B. Option 2

   C. Option 3

   D. Option 4

   E. Option 5

2. If you decide that returning to Newark quickly is no longer important, which option best matches your remaining criteria: 1) having time for dinner in New Orleans; and 2) a low price?

   A. Option 1

   B. Option 2

   C. Option 3

   D. Option 4

   E. Option 5

Typical Fat intakes of Vegans, Vegetarians and Omnivores

	Recommended Intakes	Average Intakes of a Vegan (eats no animal foods)	Average Intakes of an Ovo-Lacto Vegetarian (eats eggs and dairy)	Average Intakes of an Omnivore (eats fish and red meat)
Total Fat	15–30%	30%	32%	35%
Cholesterol	Less than 300 mg	0	150 mg	300 mg
Saturated Fat	Less than 8%	6%	10%	12%
Trans Fat	0%	1%	3%	6%
Omega–6	4%	11%	9%	6%
Omega–3	1–2%	0.75%	0.75%	0.75%

Fat Content of Selected Protein-rich Foods
(% of total fat)

Nuts and Seeds	Saturated Fat	Mono. Fat	Omega–6	Omega–3
Almonds, 1 oz.	10%	65%	23%	1%
Cashews, 1 oz	20%	59%	17%	0%
Flaxseed, 2 Tbsp	9%	18%	16%	57%
Peanuts, 1 oz.	14%	15%	32%	0%
Walnuts, 1 oz.	6%	14%	58%	14%
Animal foods				
Eggs, 1 large	31%	38%	12%	0.7%
High-fat fish, 3 oz.	20%	50%	2%	23%
Low-fat fish, 3 oz.	20%	20%	6%	50%

3. As a nutritionist, you advise patients to limit their intake of saturated fat. Which type of diet might you recommend and why?

   A. ovo-lacto vegetarian, because the average vegetarian's intake of saturated fat is 10 percent

   B. vegan, because the average vegan's intake of saturated fat is 12 percent

   C. ovo-lacto vegetarian, because the average vegetarian's intake of saturated fat is 12 percent

   D. vegan, because the average vegan's intake of saturated fat is 6 percent

   E. omnivore, because the average omnivore's intake of saturated fat is 12 percent

4. Based on the recommended and average intakes of omega-3, which foods might you decide to recommend for your patients?

   A. almonds for vegans and vegetarians; eggs for vegetarians and omnivores

   B. flaxseed for vegans and vegetarians; high-fat fish for omnivores

   C. cashews for vegans and vegetarians; high-fat fish for omnivores

   D. peanuts for vegans and vegetarians; high-fat fish for omnivores

   E. walnuts for vegans; eggs for vegetarians; high-fat fish for omnivores

ANSWER KEY

Item 1:   **C** Option 3

Item 2:   **D** Option 4

Item 3:   **D** vegan, because the average vegan's intake of saturated fat is 6 percent and many non-animal proteins are relatively low in saturated fat

Item 4:   **A** almonds for vegans and vegetarians; eggs for vegetarians and omnivores

APPLIED MATHEMATICS

Using applied mathematics will help you succeed in a health science career. The mathematics required for some jobs in this cluster can be very complex, but basic math skills will come in handy for most careers. Some skills are very simple, such as counting out pills to fill prescriptions. In other cases you may need to use several mathematical steps to calculate a profit margin. Some key skills include multiplying and dividing, finding percentages, and adding fractions.

In the following pages, you will encounter a variety of applied math problems. Each item describes a real-life situation in a health science career. You will be asked to solve the problems by applying your mathematical skills. You may need to use arithmetic, geometry, or measurement skills, for example.

When you read a question on the following pages, think about what is being asked and how you might find the answer. Read the problem carefully, focusing on the information you are asked to find or the steps you are asked to take. After you have chosen an answer, look back to make sure you have answered the question being asked.

By learning and practicing these key mathematical skills, you will put yourself in a better position to succeed in the health science industry.

KEY SKILLS FOR CAREER SUCCESS

Here are the topics and skills covered in this section and some examples how you might use them to solve workplace problems.

TOPIC	SKILL
Perform Basic Arithmetic Calculations to Solve Workplace Problems	1. Solve Problems with Whole Numbers and Negative Numbers 2. Use Fractions, Decimals, and Percentages to Solve Workplace Problems

Example: As a pharmacist, you may need to use fractions, decimals, and percentages when dispensing medications.

TOPIC	SKILL
Apply Computations to Solve Workplace Problems	3. Use General Problem Solving 4. Solve Problems in Geometry

Example: As a biomedical engineer, you may need to calculate areas and perimeters when devising new medical equipment.

TOPIC	SKILL
Solve Measurement Problems	5. Calculate with Conversions and Formulas 6. Manipulate Formulas to Solve Problems

Example: As a nurse, you may be required to use conversions and formulas when reading patients' vital signs.

TOPIC	SKILL
Make Spending Decisions to Solve Workplace Problems	7. Calculate Costs and Discounts 8. Make Consumer Comparisons

Example: As a home health aide, you may need to calculate costs and comparison shop when helping a patient purchase food and other necessities.

SOLVE PROBLEMS WITH WHOLE NUMBERS AND NEGATIVE NUMBERS

Addition, subtraction, multiplication, and division of whole numbers are important skills in any career cluster, and health science is no exception. A dental assistant, for example, may need to use multiplication to figure out how many dental instruments to sterilize. A head nurse may use division to help assign nurses on a shift to the number of patients in a unit.

1. Working as a dental assistant, you will sterilize and disinfect a set of 5 instruments for each patient. The dentist is scheduled to see 14 patients today. How many instruments will you be disinfecting?

   A. 55

   B. 60

   C. 70

   D. 75

   E. 85

2. You are a personal trainer at a health club where you train members to learn the proper way to use the equipment. On Monday, you have 5 clients; on Tuesday 1 client; on Wednesday 8 clients; on Thursday 5 clients; and on Friday 3 clients. How many clients did you work with on those 5 days?

   A. 22

   B. 24

   C. 26

   D. 28

   E. 30

3. As a medical receptionist for a pediatrician, you must coordinate appointments to examine children for their school records. This morning, 14 children are in the waiting room. After the pediatrician has seen 9 children, how many children are still in the waiting room?

   A. 4

   B. 5

   C. 6

   D. 7

   E. 8

4. One major responsibility you have as a head nurse is to oversee the care provided by the floor nurses for all patients on the third floor of the hospital. There are 64 rooms on the third floor. Each nurse is responsible for the patients in 8 rooms. How many nurses are needed on the third floor?

   A. 3

   B. 4

   C. 7

   D. 8

   E. 12

5. You are a nutritionist's assistant. One of your duties is to inform patients on how to safely prepare meat. To safely consume pork, it must first be heated to 71°Celsius. To safely freeze pork, it must be brought down to –18°Celsius. What is the difference between the temperature at which pork is safely frozen and the temperature at which pork is safely cooked?

   A. 53°C

   B. 89°C

   C. 101°C

   D. 115°C

   E. 121°C

6. You work in a medical supply warehouse. As the company's bookkeeper, it is your job to compute the balances of your company's clients. You have just received a check from one of your top clients, Dr. Kuperman, for $5,000. Before receiving this check, Dr. Kuperman's balance was $12,000. What is Dr. Kuperman's balance after receiving this check?

   A. –$17,000

   B. –$7,000

   C. $7,000

   D. $17,000

   E. $70,000

7. As a medical secretary, you maintain records and pay bills for a therapist. It is the end of the month and time to pay bills. There is a balance of $5,425 in the checkbook, and the total amount billed is $6,330. What will be the balance after paying the bills?

   A. –$850

   B. –$875

   C. –$890

   D. –$900

   E. –$905

8. You are a school nurse aide. You have to sterilize a reusable cold pack after each use by bringing it to 100° Celsius. Afterwards, you need to freeze the cold pack so it can be reused. To freeze the cold pack, it must be brought down –12° Celsius. What is the difference in temperature from when the cold pack has been sterilized to when the cold pack has been refrozen?

   A. –112°C

   B. –8°C

   C. –12°C

   D. 12°C

   E. 112°C

ANSWER KEY

Item 1: **C** 5 × 14 = 70 instruments

Item 2: **A** 5 + 1 + 8 + 5 + 3 = 22 clients

Item 3: **B** 14 − 9 = 5 children

Item 4: **D** 64 ÷ 8 = 8 nurses

Item 5: **B** 71 − (−18) = 89° Celsius

Item 6: **C** 12,000 + (−5,000) = $7,000

Item 7: **E** −6,330 + 5,425 = −$905

Item 8: **E** 100 − (−12) = 112° Celsius

2

USE FRACTIONS, DECIMALS, AND PERCENTAGES TO SOLVE WORKPLACE PROBLEMS

In the health science industry, workers come across quantities represented in many different ways. For example, dietetic technicians need to know how to portion meal sizes for patients with different caloric needs. The ability to perform workplace calculation using different forms of numbers is an important workplace skill.

1. You are the assistant to a speech language pathologist who is working at an elementary school. Testing showed that, of the 100 children in the third grade class, 12 percent need some type of treatment. How many children need treatment?

   A. 1

   B. 3

   C. 12

   D. 15

   E. 20

2. As a clinical data manager, you record staffing information. During the last two weeks, one doctor worked $21\frac{1}{2}$ hours and $22\frac{1}{4}$ hours, respectively. You must enter the total number of hours worked as a decimal number. What number do you enter?

   A. 41.00

   B. 42.50

   C. 43.00

   D. 43.75

   E. 44.75

3. You are a podiatrist's assistant reviewing the doctor's schedule for next week. The doctor is scheduled for surgery for $4\frac{1}{2}$ hours on three days during the week. How much time is the podiatrist scheduled for surgery?

   A. $12\frac{1}{2}$

   B. 13

   C. $13\frac{1}{2}$

   D. 14

   E. $14\frac{1}{2}$

4. In your job as a physical therapist's assistant, you administer therapeutic exercises and massages, among other duties. You earn $10 per hour and work $7\frac{1}{2}$ hours per day. How much do you earn in one day?

   A. $60

   B. $65

   C. $70

   D. $75

   E. $80

5. As a music therapist you run a program for seniors for whom you play recordings of their favorite music. Show tunes make up $\frac{1}{2}$ of the program and "oldies" make up $\frac{1}{3}$ of the program. The remaining portion of the program is spent discussing the lyrics of one song. You keep track of the time spent on each activity so you know how to adjust the program based on participant feedback. How much of the music therapy program consists of playing recorded music?

A. $\frac{3}{6}$

B. $\frac{5}{6}$

C. $\frac{7}{8}$

D. $\frac{11}{12}$

E. $\frac{13}{14}$

6. As a nurse working in a hospice facility, you care for patients who are terminally ill. Your main responsibility is to make patients as comfortable as possible and minimize their pain for their remaining days. To prevent dehydration, you track the amount of water patients drink each day. Today, one patient drank $\frac{3}{4}$ glass in the morning; $\frac{1}{2}$ glass at noon; $\frac{1}{2}$ glass at dinner time; and $\frac{3}{4}$ glass before bedtime. How many glasses of water did the patient drink today?

A. 2

B. $2\frac{1}{4}$

C. $2\frac{1}{2}$

D. $2\frac{3}{4}$

E. 3

7. You are working as a critical care nurse's assistant, assigned to the geriatric section of the hospital. You need to track your hours on a time sheet. You spend $1\frac{1}{4}$ hours in doing paperwork, $2\frac{1}{2}$ hours with patients before lunch, and $2\frac{3}{4}$ hours with patients in the afternoon. How many hours do you spend with patients?

A. 5

B. $5\frac{1}{4}$

C. $5\frac{3}{4}$

D. 6

E. $6\frac{1}{2}$

8. As a school dietitian, you recommend a soy milk that lists the following per serving information on its Nutrition Facts panel: saturated fat 0.5 grams, trans fat 0 grams, polyunsaturated fat 3 grams, and monounsaturated fat 1 grams. How much total fat does this soy milk contain per serving?

A. 3.1 grams

B. 3.5 grams

C. 4 grams

D. 4.5 grams

E. 5 grams

ANSWER KEY

Item 1: **C** 12% × 100 = 12 children

Item 2: **D** $21\frac{1}{2} + 22\frac{1}{4} = 21.50 + 22.25 = 43.75$ hours

Item 3: **C** $4\frac{1}{2} \times 3 = \frac{9}{2} \times \frac{3}{1} = \frac{27}{2} = 13\frac{1}{2}$

Item 4: **D** $\$10 \times 7\frac{1}{2}$ hours $= \frac{10}{1} \times \frac{15}{2} = \frac{150}{2} = \$75$

Item 5: **B** $\frac{1}{2} + \frac{1}{3} = \frac{3}{6} + \frac{2}{6} = \frac{5}{6}$

Item 6: **C** $\frac{3}{4} + \frac{1}{2} + \frac{1}{2} + \frac{3}{4} = \frac{6}{8} + \frac{4}{8} + \frac{4}{8} + \frac{6}{8} = \frac{20}{8} = 2\frac{4}{8} = 2\frac{1}{2}$ glasses

Item 7: **B** $2\frac{1}{2} + 2\frac{3}{4} = 2\frac{2}{4} + 2\frac{3}{4} = 4\frac{5}{4} = 5\frac{1}{4}$ hours

Item 8: **D** 0.5 + 3.0 + 1.0 = 4.5 grams

USE GENERAL PROBLEM SOLVING

Perform Basic
Arithmetic
Calculations
to Solve
Workplace
Problems

**Apply
Computations
to Solve
Workplace
Problems**

Solve
Measurement
Problems

Make Spending
Decisions
to Solve
Workplace
Problems

Some mathematical calculations require more than one operation. An emergency room nurse might have to keep track of the number of patients seen each day, find the average number of patients seen per day, and use that average to determine staffing needs. Being able to quickly perform such calculations can improve a health science worker's efficiency.

1. You work as an assistant to an audiologist. Your office originally had 10 appointments scheduled for tomorrow. This morning, 2 patients called in to cancel their appointments, and a new patient called to make an appointment. How many appointments are now scheduled for tomorrow?

   A. 2

   B. 5

   C. 9

   D. 10

   E. 12

2. As an aide to a naturopathic physician, you are helping a patient understand her prescription. The prescription indicates 4 herb capsules and 2 botanical extract capsules are to be taken each day. How many capsules will the patient be taking in a week?

   A. 34

   B. 36

   C. 38

   D. 40

   E. 42

3. You are a health educator planning to give a talk on sexually transmitted diseases to a school group of 30 junior high school students, 60 parents, and 2 teachers. You have been asked to provide printed copies of your talk to each participant. Your talk is 5 pages long. How many sheets of paper will you need?

   A. 305

   B. 370

   C. 460

   D. 510

   E. 575

4. You are an assistant to a chiropractor and are responsible for the office bookkeeping. This afternoon, you are going to pay bills and make a deposit at the bank. The bills are: $300.28 to the phone company, $235.00 to the computer service, $175.50 to electric company, and $235.10 for office insurance. The deposit is $670.00. You have $1,275.33 in the office account. What will be the account balance after the bills are paid and the deposit made?

   A. $923.95

   B. $946.58

   C. $975.6

   D. $999.45

   E. $1,201.22

5. You are a massage therapist who designs treatments that incorporate an optional whirlpool bath. Each massage takes 45 minutes, then the client goes into the whirlpool bath for 15 minutes. On one day you saw 8 clients. Three did not want to use the whirlpool. How much total time did your clients spend getting treatment?

   A. 6.75 hours

   B. 7 hours

   C. 7.25 hours

   D. 8 hours

   E. 8.25 hours

6. You work as a veterinary assistant. Part of your job is to walk the dogs on a regular basis. Your office has 4 golden retrievers, 3 Boston terriers, 2 poodles, and a pug. The golden retrievers and poodles require 2 walks per day. The terriers and pug require 1 walk. Assuming you walk each dog individually, how many walks will you take in a day?

   A. 3

   B. 6

   C. 16

   D. 20

   E. 21

7. As a medical illustrator, you are setting up an exhibit for a training session for a group of pediatricians learning about new diagnostic and treatment methods. When setting up the room, you need to distribute the artwork among 4 walls. You have 6 black and white illustrations for each wall and 4 colored photos for each wall. Which expression shows the number of pieces of art to be hung?

   A. 4×6

   B. $4 + 4 + 6$

   C. $(4 + 4) \times 6$

   D. $4 \times (6 + 4)$

   E. $6 + 4$

8. You are a radiology technologist who this week took chest X-rays. You took 11 sets of X-rays of teens, 6 more of women than was taken of teens, and 4 more of men than women. How many chest X-rays of men did you take that week?

   A. 19

   B. 21

   C. 23

   D. 25

   E. 27

ANSWER KEY

Item 1: **C** 10 − 2 = 8; 8 + 1 = 9 appointments

Item 2: **E** 4 + 2 = 6; 6 × 7 = 42 capsules

Item 3: **C** 30 + 60 + 2 = 92; 92 × 5 = 460 sheets

Item 4: **D** 300.28 + 235.00 + 175.50 = 945.88; 1,275.33 − 945.88 = 329.45; 329.45 + 670.00 = $999.45

Item 5: **C** 45 + 15 = 60; 8 − 3 = 5; (5 × 60) + (3 × 45) = 300 + 135 = 435; 435 ÷ 60 = 7.25 hours

Item 6: **C** 4 + 2 = 6; 3 + 1 = 4; (6 × 2) + (4 × 1) = 12 + 4 = 16 walks

Item 7: **D** 4 × (6 + 4) = 4 × 10 = 40

Item 8: **B** 11 + 6 = 17; 17 + 4 = 21 men's chest X-rays

SOLVE PROBLEMS IN GEOMETRY

Perform Basic
Arithmetic
Calculations
to Solve
Workplace
Problems

**Apply
Computations
to Solve
Workplace
Problems**

Solve
Measurement
Problems

Make Spending
Decisions
to Solve
Workplace
Problems

Knowing how to determine the perimeters and areas of objects and spaces, from hospital rooms to laboratory containers to medical equipment, is an important skill in the health science industry. It is important to be able to find the perimeter of both circles and rectangles.

1. As a medical facilities manager at a rehabilitation center, you are ordering new beds. You order regular beds since most of your patients do not require bedrails. But for the few patients that need extra safety, you order separate rails that can be attached to the regular beds. You order enough railings to fit around 8 beds. The beds are 9 feet long by 4 feet wide. How much railing material will you need to fit around the 8 beds?

    A. 190 feet

    B. 195 feet

    C. 198 feet

    D. 202 feet

    E. 208 feet

2. As a clinic manager, you are working with a contractor to order new floor covering for a laboratory. The lab measures 25 feet long × 20 feet wide. What is the area you need to cover with the new floor?

    A. 400 square feet

    B. 425 square feet

    C. 450 square feet

    D. 500 square feet

    E. 550 square feet

3. You are a medical illustrator preparing an exhibit of anatomical illustrations for a university medical museum. You have 6 illustrations and each needs a new wooden frame. All the illustrations are the same size: 15 inches long by 12 inches wide. They do not require mats. How much framing material is needed for all 6 illustrations?

    A. 314 inches

    B. 324 inches

    C. 334 inches

    D. 340 inches

    E. 354 inches

4. Working as an assistant to a biotechnologist, you have been asked to order new custom adhesive labels for several metal storage containers. The containers are 4 inches in diameter and 8 inches tall. The label should cover the entire surface of the container with no overlap. What are the dimensions of the label?

    A. 8 inches × 8 inches

    B. 8 inches × 9.45 inches

    C. 8 inches × 11.6 inches

    D. 8 inches × 12.56 inches

    E. 8 inches × 16.23 inches

5. You are a hospital facilities manager who must replace the linoleum floor covering in a storage room that measures 9 feet wide on all sides. You have to know the square footage to get a price estimate. What is the area of the storage room?

    A. 18 square feet

    B. 27 square feet

    C. 36 square feet

    D. 81 square feet

    E. 118 square feet

6. You are an animal technician helping a veterinarian replace several cages that are in disrepair. The cage sizes are non-standard and must be custom built. You must replace 5 large cages (4 yards per side) and 5 small cages (2 yards per side). What is the total length of the cage walls for all cages?

    A. 120 yards

    B. 125 yards

    C. 130 yards

    D. 135 yards

    E. 140 yards

7. As a facilities manager for a hospital, you must make sure all floor surfaces are clean and in good condition. You periodically buff and polish the marble floor of the hospital lobby. To make sure you have enough polishing wax, you must know the area of the floor. If the floor measures 80 feet by 50 feet, what is the area of the floor?

    A. 3,500 square feet

    B. 4,000 square feet

    C. 4,050 square feet

    D. 4,500 square feet

    E. 5,000 square feet

8. You are an optometrist helping create a table for an eyeglass display. You want to create a triangular table to be placed flush against the walls in a corner of the office. The table sides placed against the walls should be 4 feet long. What will be the surface area of the table top?

    A. 6 square feet

    B. 6.5 square feet

    C. 7 square feet

    D. 7.5 square feet

    E. 8 square feet

ANSWER KEY

Item 1: **E** $2 \times (9 + 4) = 2 \times 13 = 26$; $26 \times 8 = 208$ feet

Item 2: **D** $25 \times 20 = 500$ square feet

Item 3: **B** $2 \times (15 + 12) = 54$; $54 \times 6 = 324$ inches

Item 4: **D** $3.14 \times 4 = 12.56$ inches; 8 inches $\times 12.56$ inches

Item 5: **D** 9 feet $\times 9$ feet $= 81$ square feet

Item 6: **A** $2 \times 4 = 8$; $4 \cdot 4 = 16$; $(16 \times 5) + (8 \times 5) = 80 + 40 = 120$ yards

Item 7: **B** $80 \times 50 = 4,000$ square feet

Item 8: **E** $4 \times 4 = 16$; $\frac{16}{2} = 8$ square feet

CALCULATE WITH CONVERSIONS AND FORMULAS

Some calculations in the health science industry may require using conversions and formulas. A laboratory assistant may need to use the formula for calculating density to make sure the concentration of a laboratory chemical is accurate, for example. Other calculations require converting US measurements to metric, such as converting teaspoons to milliliters.

1. You are working as an assistant to an optician, helping a client choose a frame for a new pair of glasses. He decides on a frame that costs $310.50. He pays with $320.00 in cash. What combination of money would be the correct change?

   A. 1 five-dollar bill, 3 one-dollar bills, 1 quarter

   B. 1 five-dollar bill, 4 one-dollar bills, 2 quarters

   C. 2 five-dollar bills

   D. 2 five-dollar bills, 2 quarters

   E. 1 five-dollar bill, 6 one-dollar bills, 1 quarter

2. As a pharmacy technician, you price and file the filled prescriptions. The pharmacist filled 45 prescriptions, and it should take you 5 minutes to price and file each. How long will the project take?

   A. 3 hours, 45 minutes

   B. 4 hours

   C. 4 hours, 15 minutes

   D. 5 hours

   E. 5 hours, 15 minutes

3. Working in a hospital as a registered nurse, you need to monitor medications. One patient needs a pill every 4 hours. You gave the last dose at 10 a.m. At what time should you give the next dose?

   A. 12 p.m.

   B. 2 p.m.

   C. 12 a.m.

   D. 2 a.m.

   E. 4 a.m.

4. As the health services manager, you track your time spent in meetings to better plan your schedule. The first day, you met with the Clerical Unit for 2 hours, Business Affairs for $1\frac{3}{4}$ hours, and Personnel for 1 hour. The second day, you met with Maintenance for 45 minutes, Equipment for $1\frac{1}{4}$ hour, and Marketing for $1\frac{1}{2}$ hours. What was the total time spent in all meetings?

   A. 7 hours, 15 minutes

   B. 7 hours, 30 minutes

   C. 7 hours, 45 minutes

   D. 8 hours

   E. 8 hours, 15 minutes

5. As an assistant to a pediatrician, you work with infants and small children. One of the infants under your care weighed 8 pounds, 3 ounces at birth. For the first 6 months of his life, he gains 20 ounces each month. What is the infant's weight at 6 months?

   A. 14 pounds, 6 ounces

   B. 15 pounds, 7 ounces

   C. 15 pounds, 11 ounces

   D. 16 pounds, 1 ounce

   E. 16 pounds, 6 ounces

6. You work as an aide to a dermatologist who sells facial products in his office. A customer purchases a 12-ounce bottle of face wash for $9.00, a 4-ounce tube of face cream at $14.00, and an 8-ounce tube of sunscreen at $17.50. What is the total cost of the products (not including tax)?

   A. $38.50

   B. $39.00

   C. $40.50

   D. $42.00

   E. $43.50

7. As an aide working with an internist, you check patients' vital signs. Your current patient weighs 270 pounds, has a blood pressure of 140 over 90, and a temperature of 98.6 degrees Fahrenheit. His last appointment was 6 months ago. If he lost an average of 5 pounds each month, how much did he weigh at his previous appointment?

   A. 285 pounds

   B. 290 pounds

   C. 295 pounds

   D. 300 pounds

   E. 305 pounds

8. As an assistant to a rehabilitation physician, you help schedule patients' treatments. Today's schedule includes a 30-minute ultraviolet radiation treatment at 9:30 a.m., a 15-minute physical therapy session at 10:30 a.m., a 30-minute heat treatment at 11:30 a.m., and a 45-minute consultation with a patient and the doctor at 1:00 p.m. How much time is unscheduled between 9:00 a.m. and 12:00 noon?

   A. 1 hour, 15 minutes

   B. 1 hour, 30 minutes

   C. 1 hour, 45 minutes

   D. 2 hours

   E. 2 hours, 15 minutes

ANSWER KEY

Item 1: **B** $320.00 - 310.50 = \$9.50 = $ (1 five-dollar bill, 4 one-dollar bills, 2 quarters)

Item 2: **A** $45 \times 5 = 225 = $ 3 hours and 45 minutes

Item 3: **B** 10 a.m. + 4 hours = 2 p.m.

Item 4: **E** $(2 \times 60) + (1\frac{3}{4} \times 60) + (1 \times 60) + 45 + (1\frac{1}{4} \times 60) + (1\frac{1}{2} \times 60) = 120 + 105 + 60 + 45 + 75 + 90 = 495$. $\frac{495}{60} = $ 8 hours and 15 minutes

Item 5: **C** 8 pounds, 3 ounces $= (8 \times 16) + 3 = 131$; $20 \times 6 = 120$; $131 + 120 = 251$; $251 \div 16 = 15.7$; = 15 pounds and 11 ounces

Item 6: **C** $9.00 + 14.00 + 17.50 = \$40.50$

Item 7: **D** $5 \times 6 = 30$; $270 + 30 = 300$ pounds

Item 8: **A** $30 + 15 + 30 = 75$; $180 - 75 = 105 \div 60 = $ 1 hour and 45 minutes

PULATE FORMULAS
LVE PROBLEMS

...s in the health science, a formula may need to be
... a problem. For example, a family practitioner or nurse
... to use a formula to calculate the correct dosage of a
... the patient's weight. Health science workers should be
... with formulas to find the information required.

1. You are a laboratory assistant preparing a solution of a liquid chemical. You need to measure out 50 grams of a chemical whose density is 2 grams per milliliter. What is the volume of the chemical needed for your solution? The formula for mass: mass = density × volume.

   A. 10 milliliters

   B. 25 milliliters

   C. 50 milliliters

   D. 100 milliliters

   E. 150 milliliters

2. You are a medical equipment sales clerk. A client wants to purchase an MRI machine that is 10 feet tall. You need to make sure the machine will fit in a designated room. The floor of the room is 20 feet by 30 feet. The volume of the room is 6,000 cubic feet. How tall is the room?

   A. 8 feet

   B. 9 feet

   C. 9.5 feet

   D. 10 feet

   E. 15 feet

3. You are a sports physical therapist helping a baseball player recover from a knee injury. The baseball player is running around a circular track that is 400 meters around. Even though the baseball player is injured, he runs too fast for you to keep up and you have to run across the diameter of the circular path. About how many meters do you run when you are running across the diameter?

   A. 86 meters

   B. 100 meters

   C. 127 meters

   D. 800 meters

   E. 1,256 meters

4. As a pharmacy technician, you prepare prescription labels for medication that is dispensed. One children's liquid medication is prescribed for 3 teaspoons per dose, 4 times a day. The liquid-measuring syringe that you provide with the medicine measures in milliliters. If 5 milliliters = 1 teaspoon, how much medicine should the child receive per day?

   A. 2.4 milliliters

   B. 12 milliliters

   C. 15 milliliters

   D. 20 milliliters

   E. 60 milliliters

5. As a hospital maintenance engineer at a hospital that is exploring green technology, you are asked to provide information about the energy usage of some of the devices in the hospital. One device uses 120 volts of electricity and draws 5 amps of current during its use. It runs on an AC current that cycles at 60 hertz (Hz). The formula for finding watts is: *watts = (volts)(amps)*. How much power does the device use?

A. 0.04 watt

B. 10 watts

C. 24 watts

D. 600 watts

E. 36,000 watts

6. As part of your job as a medical technician, you are calculating how long an oxygen cylinder should last. To do so, you need to know the volume of the cylinder. You determine that the inside measurements are 22 inches long by 18 inches in circumference. What volume should you use for your calculations?

A. 396 cubic inches

B. 567 cubic inches

C. 622 cubic inches

D. 1,244 cubic inches

E. 5,595 cubic inches

ANSWER KEY

Item 1: **B** 50 grams = 2 grams/milliliters × volume; 50 grams ÷ (2 grams/milliliter) = 25 milliliters

Item 2: **D** 6,000 cubic feet = height × 20 feet × 30 feet. 6,000 cubic feet = height × 600; height = 10 feet

Item 3: **C** 400 meters = 3.14 × diameter; diameter = about 127 meters

Item 4: **E** 3 teaspoons × 3 doses per day = 12 teaspoons per day; 12 teaspoons × 5 = 60 milliliters per day

Item 5: **D** watts = 120 × 5 = 600 watts

Item 6: **B** *circumference ≈ 3.14 x 1 × radius*
18 ≈ 3.14 x 2 × radius
2.866 ≈ radius
volume ≈ 3.14 x (radius)² × height
volume ≈ 3.14 x (2.866)² × 22
volume ≈ 3.14 x 8.2139 × 22
volume ≈ 567.42 inches³ or 567 cubic inches rounded to the nearest whole number

Perform Basic
Arithmetic
Calculations
to Solve
Workplace
Problems

Apply
Computations
to Solve
Workplace
Problems

Solve
Measurement
Problems

**Make
Spending
Decisions
to Solve
Workplace
Problems**

CALCULATE COSTS AND DISCOUNTS

Many jobs in the health science industry require workers to calculate costs and discounts. A certified dietary manager, for example, may need to calculate the cost of buying foods including discounts for bulk items for a hospital cafeteria. These skills are important for budgeting and collecting payments.

1. You are an office assistant for a periodontist. The office is running out of its brochure on proper gum care. Your local printer charges $0.25 for 1 brochure and offers a 15 percent discount for any quantity over 1,000. How much will 1,500 brochures cost?

   A. $300.25

   B. $320.50

   C. $350.00

   D. $356.25

   E. $375.00

2. As an assistant to a speech language pathologist, you are helping to create a DVD to show to new patients and their families. Your chosen videographer charges a rate of $120 per hour and a 10 percent extra charge for work that goes beyond 8 hours in one day. She estimates the job will take 10 hours. You prefer to shoot the video in one day. How much will it cost?

   A. $1,125

   B. $1,200

   C. $1,224

   D. $1,300

   E. $1,352

3. As a genetics counselor, you are planning to attend a conference in Atlanta with two counselors you work with. Yesterday the price was $375.00 per person. However, when calling to make the reservation today, you learned that the price had gone up 5 percent. This includes all fees and taxes. What will be the total cost for the 3 tickets?

   A. $1,081.00

   B. $1,181.25

   C. $1,281.25

   D. $1,300.00

   E. $1,381.25

4. You are a dental hygienist preparing to reorder lab coats for the office. When you last ordered lab coats, you paid $700 for one box of 50 coats. Your supplier has since increased the price of lab coats by 15 percent since your last order. You need to order 150 lab coats. How much will they cost?

   A. $1,990

   B. $2,105

   C. $2,275

   D. $2,415

   E. $2,550

5. As an ophthalmic medical technologist, you just received a notice from the laboratory that makes contact lenses that they need to increase their prices by 20 percent. You normally charge $225 for a pair of contact lenses. If you raise your prices by the same percentage as the lab's increase, how much will your customers be paying for contact lenses?

A. $270

B. $272

C. $274

D. $276

E. $278

6. You are a medical office manager reviewing staff salaries at the end of the year. You are considering a 5 percent raise for three of your staff. Last year the nurse's aide received $29.000; the assistant office manager, $35,000; and the central service technician, $28,000. By how much will your department need to increase their salary budget next year if all three workers were given the 5 percent increase?

A. $4,100

B. $4,220

C. $4,600

D. $4,820

E. $4,900

7. As a purchasing manager, you are responsible for buying supplies for a community health clinic. Your supplier has raised the shipping fee by 10% for orders under $100. The fee was $4.50. You place an order for $85 of supplies. How much will the order cost with shipping?

A. $80.05

B. $80.50

C. $89.50

D. $89.95

E. $93.50

8. You are an occupational safety specialist. You are putting together a training video on workplace safety. To create the video, you need to rent video equipment for 10 days. The charge per day for the equipment is $159. Because you are renting the equipment for more than 5 days, you will receive a 10% discount on the total cost of the rental. How much will you pay?

A. $159.00

B. $715.50

C. $1,431.00

D. $1,510.50

E. $1,590.00

ANSWER KEY

Item 1: **D** $1,000 \times .25 = \$250$; $500 \times .25 = 125$; $125 - (125 \times 15\%) = 106.25$; $250 + 106.25 = \$356.25$

Item 2: **C** $8 \times 120 = 960$; $10 - 8 = 2$; $2 \times 120 = 240$; $240 + (240 \times 10\%) = 264$; $960 + 264 = \$1,224$

Item 3: **B** $375 + (375 \times 5\%) = 393.75$; $393.75 \times 3 = \$1,181.25$

Item 4: **D** $700 + (700 \times 15\%) = 805$; $150 \div 50 = 3$; $805 \times 3 = \$2,415$

Item 5: **A** $225.00 + (225.00 \times 20\%) = \$270$

Item 6: **C** $(29,000 + 35,000 + 28,000) \times 5\% = \$4,600$

Item 7: **D** $4.50 + (4.50 \times 10\%) = 4.50 + 0.45 = 4.95$; $85 + 4.95 = \$89.95$

Item 8: **C** $159 \times 10 = 1,590$; $1,590 - (1,590 \times 10\%) = 1,590 - 159 = \$1,431.00$

MAKE CONSUMER COMPARISONS

Health science workers who make purchasing decisions or recommendations must often make calculations that compare two or more purchasing options. A dental hygienist may need to compare the costs of dental office supplies from various suppliers, while a health services manager may compare the cost of training programs for hospital staff. Being able to make these calculations and find the best deal is an important skill in this industry.

1. You are an assistant to a sports physical therapist. You are helping find the best pricing for jumping ropes. Vendor A sells them in boxes of a dozen for $18.00 per box and gives a 10 percent discount per box. Vendor B sells them in packages of 3 at $4.50 per package. If you choose the vendor with the best price, how much will you pay for 48 jumping ropes?

   A. $61.50
   B. $62.40
   C. $64.80
   D. $67.00
   E. $69.90

2. As a certified dietary manager at a hospital, you are about to place a large order for nonperishable foods. Supplier 1 has a price of $5,600 plus $200 shipping. Supplier 2 has a price of $5,275 plus $250 for shipping. Assuming the quality is no different, how much will you pay if you choose the vendor with the lowest total price?

   A. $5,025
   B. $5,100
   C. $5,225
   D. $5,350
   E. $5,525

3. In your job as a pharmacy aide, you notice that a specific pain medicine should be reordered. Vendor A sells the medicine for $8.95 per 100-pill bottle; Vendor B charges $5.85 for a 50-pill bottle; and Vendor C charges $3.95 for a 24-pill bottle. If you choose the vendor with the best deal, how much will you pay per pill?

   A. 7 cents
   B. 8 cents
   C. 9 cents
   D. 10 cents
   E. 12 cents

4. You are a receptionist helping to find the best price for new carpet in a doctor's waiting room. The room measures 25 feet × 20 feet. Supplier A charges $11.00 per square foot plus $2.25 per square foot for padding and installation. Supplier B charges $13.00 per square foot with padding and installation included. If you choose the supplier with the lowest total price, how much will you pay?

   A. $6,000
   B. $6,225
   C. $6,350
   D. $6,500
   E. $6,525

5. As an assistant working with a hearing aid specialist, you find that you are low on a particular hearing aid model. Supplier A charges $50 each or $400 for 10. Supplier B charges $50 each or $800 for 25. You need to order 50 hearing aids. What is the least amount you can pay?

   A. $1,400

   B. $1,450

   C. $1,500

   D. $1,600

   E. $2,000

6. You are a health and safety manager. You need a supply of 1,000 disposable rubber gloves for your job. A box of 500 gloves costs $19.95, and a box of 250 gloves costs $10.95. Which is the better deal and how much do you save on 1,000 gloves?

   A. The box of 500; $0.10

   B. The box of 500; $1.00

   C. The box of 500; $3.90

   D. The box of 250; $6.10

   E. The box of 250; $9.00

7. As a clinical lab technician, one of your instruments has broken and must be replaced immediately. Company A sells the instrument for $695.00 and will charge $39.95 for overnight shipping. Company B sells the instrument for $619.95 and will charge $45.00 for shipping. Who has the better deal and by how much?

   A. Company B by $30.00

   B. Company B by $70.00

   C. Company B by $74.95

   D. Company A by $75.05

   E. Company A by $115.00

8. As a nurse, you order blood collection tubes for a lab. 104 boxes of tubes are used in one year. Two suppliers offer the type of tube your lab needs. Supplier A sells 10 boxes for $109 and 25 boxes for $265. Supplier B sells 20 boxes for $214, 50 boxes for $525, and 150 boxes for $1, 530. What is the lowest price you could pay for a year's supply?

   A. $1,050

   B. $1,159

   C. $1,169

   D. $1,199

   E. $1,284

ANSWER KEY

Item 1: **C** 48 ÷ 12 = 4; 4 × 18 = 72; 72 – 72 × 10% = $64.80; 48 ÷ 3 = 16; 4.50 × 16 = $72.00

Item 2: **E** 5,600 + 200 = 5,800; 5,275 + 250 = $5,525; $5,525 is the best price.

Item 3: **C** 8.95 ÷ 100 = $0.09 for Vendor A; 5.85 ÷ 50 = $0.12 for Vendor B; 3.95 ÷ 24 = $0.16 for Vendor C; The best price is from Vendor A at 9 cents per pill.

Item 4: **D** 25 x 20 = 500; (11.00 + 2.25) × 500 = 13.25 × 500 = $6,625; 13.00 × 500 = $6,500

Item 5: **D** Supplier A: 50 ÷ 10 = 5; 400 × 5 = 2,000; Supplier B: 50 ÷ 25 hearing aids = 2; 800 × 2 = 1,600; Supplier B is the best deal at $1,600 for 50 hearing aids.

Item 6: **C** 1,000 ÷ 500 = 2; 19.95 × 2 = 39.90; 1,000 ÷ 250 = 4; 10.95 × 4 = 43.80; 39.90 < 43.80; 43.80 – 39.90 = 3.90

Item 7: **B** 695.00 + 39.95 = 734.95; 619.95 + 45.00 = 664.95; 734.95 – 664.95 = $70.00

Item 8: **C** 104 ÷ 25 = 4.16, so 4 boxes of 25 or 4 × 25 = 100 boxes; 104 – 100 = 4 boxes, so 1 box of 10; (4 × 265) + (1 × 109) = 1,169 for Supplier A
104 ÷ 50 = 2.08, so 2 boxes of 50 or 2 × 50 = 100 boxes; 104 – 100 = 4 boxes, so 1 box of 20; (2 × 525) + (1 × 214) = 1,264 for Supplier B; 1,169 < 1,264

CAREER CLUSTERS AND PATHWAYS

A **career cluster** is a grouping of jobs and industries based on common characteristics. A **career pathway** is an area of focus within a career cluster. You can explore each of the following career clusters and pathways in McGraw-Hill Workforce's *Career Companion* series.

Agriculture, Food & Natural Resources

Food Products and Processing Systems

Plant Systems

Animal Systems

Power, Structural & Technical Systems

Natural Resources Systems

Environmental Service Systems

Agribusiness Systems

Architecture & Construction

Design/Pre-Construction

Construction

Maintenance/Operations

Arts, Audio/Video Technology & Communications

Audio and Video Technology and Film

Printing Technology

Visual Arts

Performing Arts

Journalism and Broadcasting

Telecommunications

Business Management & Administration

General Management

Business Information Management

Human Resources Management

Operations Management

Administrative Support

Education & Training

Administration and Administrative Support

Professional Support Services

Teaching/Training

Finance

Securities & Investments

Business Finance

Accounting

Insurance

Banking Services

Government & Public Administration

Governance

National Security

Foreign Service

Planning

Revenue and Taxation

Regulation

Public Management and Administration

Health Science

Therapeutic Services

Diagnostic Services

Health Informatics

Support Services

Biotechnology Research and Development

Hospitality & Tourism

Restaurants and Food/Beverage Services

Lodging

Travel & Tourism

Recreation, Amusements & Attractions

Human Services

Early Childhood Development & Services

Counseling & Mental Health Services

Family & Community Services

Personal Care Services

Consumer Services

Information Technology

Network Systems

Information Support and Services

Web and Digital Communications

Programming and Software Development

Law, Public Safety, Corrections & Security

Correction Services

Emergency and Fire Management Services

Security & Protective Services

Law Enforcement Services

Legal Services

Manufacturing

Production

Manufacturing Production Process Development

Maintenance, Installation & Repair

Quality Assurance

Logistics & Inventory Control

Health, Safety and Environmental Assurance

Marketing

Marketing Management

Professional Sales

Merchandising

Marketing Communications

Marketing Research

Science, Technology, Engineering & Mathematics

Engineering and Technology

Science and Math

Transportation, Distribution & Logistics

Transportation Operations

Logistics Planning and Management Services

Warehousing and Distribution Center Operations

Facility and Mobile Equipment Maintenance

Transportation Systems/Infrastructure Planning, Management and Regulation

Health, Safety and Environmental Management

Sales and Service